2-

GUIDEPOSTS

THE HIDDEN HAND OF GOD

EXTRAORDINARY ANGELIC ENCOUNTERS

THE HIDDEN HAND OF GOD

EXTRAORDINARY ANGELIC ENCOUNTERS

Surely there are in everyone's life certain connections, twists and
turns which pass awhile under the category of Chance, but at
the last, well examined, prove to be the very hand of God.
—Sir Thomas Browne

CARMEL, NEW YORK 10512

www.guidepostsbooks.com

Acknowledgments

Every attempt has been made to credit the sources of copyrighted material used in this book. If any such acknowledgment has been inadvertently omitted or miscredited, receipt of such information would be appreciated.

All materials that originally appeared in *Angels on Earth, Guideposts,* and *All Night, All Day Angels Watching Over Me* are reprinted with permission. Copyright © 1994, 1995, 1996, 1997, 1998, 1999 and 2000 by Guideposts, Carmel, New York 10512. All rights reserved.

All Scripture quotations, unless otherwise noted, are taken from *The Holy Bible, New International Version.* Copyright © 1973, 1978, 1984 International Bible Society. Used by permission of Zondervan Bible Publishers.

Scripture marked (KJV) are taken from *The King James Version of the Bible.*

"A Helping Hand" appeared in *An Angel To Watch Over Me.* Copyright © 1994 by Joan Wester Anderson. Published by Ballantine Books, a division of Random House, Inc.

"A Life-Saving Baby's Formula from an Angel," "The Angelic Employment Counselor" (published as "In Answer to His Prayers, an Angel Found Work for His Unemployed Father"), and "Warm Blankets and Christmas Money from an Angel" appeared in *Angels Over Their Shoulders* by Brad Steiger and Sherry Hansen Steiger. Copyright © 1995 by Brad Steiger and Sherry Hansen Steiger. Published by Ballantine Books, a division of Random House, Inc.

"An Angel Named Sly," "As Tall as Trees" (published as "David Lee and the Tractor"), "Mighty Warriors Dressed for Battle," and "Swing Low . . ." appeared in *A Rustle of Angels: Stories About Angels in Real Life and Scripture* by Marilynn Carlson Webber and William D. Webber. Copyright © 1994 by Marilynn Carlson Webber and William D. Webber. Published by Zondervan Publishing House.

"An Angel of My Own" by Rocco Francisco and "Mother's Helpers" by Teri Johnston appeared in *Mothers' Miracles,* compiled and edited by Jamie C. Miller, Laura Lewis, and Jennifer Basye Sander. Copyright © 1999 by Jamie C. Miller, Laura Lewis, and Jennifer Basye Sander. Published by William Morrow and Company, Inc.

"Angels with Nightsticks," "Companion Through the Storm," "The Gray Lady," and "Safely Home" (originally titled "The Beginning") appeared in *Where Angels Walk* by Joan Wester Anderson. Copyright © 1992 by Joan Wester Anderson. Published by Ballantine Books, a division of Random House, Inc.

"Cherubim, seraphim, all the angelic host. . ." by Madeleine L'Engle is from *Walking on Water: Reflections of Faith & Art.* Copyright © 1980 Crosswicks. Published by WaterBrook Press, a division of Random House, Inc.

"Christmas Angel of Hope" appeared in *There's An Angel On Your Shoulder* by Kelsey Tyler. Copyright © 1994 by Karen Kingsbury. Published by the Berkley Publishing Company.

(*continued on page 178*)

THE HIDDEN HAND OF GOD

EXTRAORDINARY ANGELIC ENCOUNTERS

Introduction. . . ix

Cherubim, seraphim, all the angelic host as they are described in Scripture, have a wild and radiant power that often takes us by surprise. They are not always gentle. They bar the entrance to Eden, so that we may never return home. They send plagues upon the Egyptians. They are messengers of God. They are winds. They are flames of fire. They are young men dressed in white.

Three of them came to Abraham to be his guests. One wrestles all night long with Jacob. They minister to Jesus after the temptations in the wilderness. They are God come to tell us something, and in the Old Testament it is obvious that God's people understand that angels are voices and appearances of the Master of the Universe Himself. To be visited by an angel is to be visited by God. To be touched by an angel is to be touched by God, and it is a terrifying experience. When the angel smote him on the thigh, Jacob limped forever after. Daniel, who had braved lions, trembled and fainted at the appearance of the Lord's angel. And John, on the Isle of Patmos, fell down as though dead.

I believe in angels, guardian angels; the angel who came to Gideon and told a shy, not very brave young man that he was a man of valor who was going to free his people; the angels who came to Jesus in the agony of the Garden. And, what is less comforting, avenging angels, destroying angels, angels who come bringing terror when any part of God's creation becomes too rebellious, too full of pride to remember that they are God's creatures. And, most fearful of all, fallen angels, angels who have left God and followed

Lucifer, and daily offer us their seductive and reasonable temptations. If we read the Bible, and if what we read has anything to do with what we believe, then we have no choice but to take angels seriously. . . . —*Madeleine L'Engle*

The word *angel* means messenger, one who serves as a courier, a representative, an agent, an envoy, or herald. We are told that angels are ministering spirits who attend God and are sent by Him to execute His will in Heaven and on earth. Angels serve God in many ways: they bring word of God's intentions, with announcements or forewarnings; they strengthen and encourage us physically, emotionally and spiritually; they protect and defend us; they deliver us from danger and harm; they serve as agents of God in answering our prayers; and they attend us at our deaths.

There are two risks we face when it comes to things angelic. The first is to accord the angels the power and authority that should only be accorded to the Creator Himself. And the second is to fail to accord angels the respect they are due as personal messengers of that same Creator. We run into serious difficulties when we veer onto either of these paths.

Oddly enough, the popularity that angels are currently enjoying has exposed us to both of these hazards. On the one hand, we may seek out angelic experiences, looking for angels at every turn, and attempt to access their power in order to enhance our lives. We may think that experiences with angels are evidence of truly being in touch with God.

On the other hand, seeing angels portrayed at every turn may numb us to the realities of the spiritual realm and close our ears to God's word that may come through one of His messengers. Angels seem to proliferate throughout our lives, decorating our greeting cards and toilet soap, coffee mugs and nightlights. Angels are so common that they become part of the white noise and chatter of our culture, and we simply tune out any of the lyrical messages that may come from these powerful creatures. Perhaps angels have simply become too familiar, causing us to feel rather patronizing when it comes to angels, so that ultimately we fail to give them their due respect.

Madeleine L'Engle reminds us that angels are not tame creatures who exist for our entertainment, pointing out that to be visited by an angel is to be visited by God Himself. The occasions of angelic visitation may be earth-changing or utterly personal. We may be so spiritually attuned that we recognize an angel from God, as did Mary and Joseph when angels came to them in dreams. Or we may need some help and encouragement to hear and see an angel, as did Balaam, whose donkey needed to tell him that an angel stood right in front of them in the road.

Angels are agents of God, performing tasks and carrying messages as God instructs. Angels bring messages from God, messages that encourage us, give us hope, and remind us that God is working in our lives. Angels guard us, protect us, and even rescue us when we are in danger. And angels bring God's provision and even His healing. Angels do not exist to do our bidding; they exist to do the bidding of God. And even as we celebrate the great goodness that these wonderful creatures bring into our lives, we never confuse the creation with the Creator.

The stories that follow chronicle a vast array of situations in which God uses angels to demonstrate His loving care for us. May each story direct our attention to the great goodness of God, so that we may sing along with the angels, "Glory to God in the highest."

Blessed be your glorious name,
and may it be exalted above all blessing and praise.
You alone are the LORD.
You made the heavens, even the highest heavens, and all their starry host,
the earth and all that is on it, the seas and all that is in them.
You give life to everything, and the multitudes of heaven worship you.
—Nehemiah 9:5-6

Chapter 1
God Sends His Angels as Messengers of Hope

When anxiety was great within me,
your consolation brought joy to my soul
—Psalm 94:19

Angels are first and foremost messengers, couriers who deliver God's messages of hope and comfort, and the very heart of an angel's work may be to bring consolation and reassurance to us when we are afraid and unsure.

Jacob met his angel just before his reunion with his brother Esau after a twenty-year estrangement caused by Jacob's swindling Esau out of his birthright. Gideon meets his angel while hiding from enemy troops and struggling to find the courage to lead the forces against them. Mary's fiancé Joseph is visited by angels when she turns up in the family way and he is contemplating discreetly breaking the engagement. Angels again guide him when it becomes necessary for the family to flee to Egypt in order to escape the deadly King Herod, and when it was safe for them to return to Israel.

In these situations and also in our lives, angels are messengers who bring instructions and assurance from God when we face the unknown and are anxious and concerned. The important result of these encounters may be not so much that Jacob limped the rest of his life, or that Gideon became a mighty warrior, or that Joseph married Mary and helped raise her son Jesus. The significance of these encounters is that God sometimes sends angels when we are upset by anxieties and worries and face difficulties we don't know how to handle. And the most important result of angelic visitations is not that we are provided with solutions to our problems, but rather that the angels help us refocus our attentions away from ourselves and onto the Creator Himself, the all-powerful One Who loves us enough to reveal Himself to us through His messengers.

The following stories tell of God's revelation through His angelic messengers, who bring reassurance when hope is lost.

> We wait in hope for the LORD;
> he is our help and our shield.
> In him our hearts rejoice,
> for we trust in his holy name.
> May your unfailing love rest upon us, O LORD,
> even as we put our hope in you.
>
> —Psalm 33:20-22

AN ANGEL NAMED SLY

WILLIAM D. WEBBER AND MARILYNN CARLSON WEBBER

Six months after the day Katie Lynn Dress was born, she was readmitted to Children's Hospital of Michigan for open-heart surgery, all eleven pounds of her. The surgery was a success. The tiny child's chest looked like a road map of stitches and scars, but she was alive. During her recovery Katie Lynn developed complications with blood clots and a week later was back in surgery. The major surgery began Friday afternoon at 1:30. By 8:30 that night she was returned to the cardiac unit. The surgery was a success, the doctor declared, and the Kress family, exhausted as they were, rejoiced. They thanked God, but their hearts still ached as they saw their little one hooked to seventeen intravenous tubes.

On Saturday the family returned to the hospital to spend time with the brave six-month-old infant. When it came time to leave, Carolyn, the mother, decided to stay with her baby a few more minutes while her husband Rob went to get the car. Their son Ryan and their daughter Tiffany decided to stop at the cafeteria to get a Coke on the way down. They all planned to meet in the hospital lobby.

Rob retrieved the car and was waiting in the lobby for his family. The lobby, usually a busy place, was quiet. For about ten minutes Rob was the only person there.

Then a bearded black man wearing a maintenance uniform stepped out from behind a large pillar. "How are you doing, Rob?" he asked, smiling.

A little startled, Rob replied, "Good, how are you?" Rob was not surprised that the stranger called him by name, for Rob Kress is the popular weathercaster for Channel 7 in Detroit, and strangers often call him by name.

"I hear that your daughter is going home tomorrow," the workman said.

Rob laughed, remembering the sick little girl he had just left. "No, she just had five more hours of surgery yesterday. They say she'll be lucky if she can go home a week from tomorrow."

"I must have misunderstood, then," the worker replied. He leaned against the pillar in his soiled maintenance uniform, a soft smile on his face, as though he knew something that Rob did not know but was too considerate to contradict a burdened father. *There is something different about this man*, Rob thought. A feeling of warmth and kindness seemed to flow from him.

"They call me Sly," he said. "You know, like Sylvester."

Rob looked down for a moment, wondering what was keeping his family so long. When he looked up he was alone. Sly was nowhere to be seen. There had not been time for him to leave the lobby. The man had simply vanished.

Carolyn came down from the hospital room. Ryan and Tiffany, their Cokes finished, found their father in the lobby. They began the drive home on I-75. Much to his surprise, Rob heard himself say, "Katie is coming home tomorrow."

"No way," Carolyn answered. She looked at her husband as if he were out of his mind. "I just talked with the nurses, and they said she will have to be in the hospital for several days."

"Katie will be coming home tomorrow," Rob repeated. His mind knew what the doctors and nurses had said, and he had seen with his own eyes how very sick Katie was, but in his heart Rob believed.

The following day, Sunday, Rob and Carolyn returned to the hospital about noon. As they walked into the cardiac unit on the sixth floor southwest, Katie's nurse Audra looked relieved. "I've been trying to reach you. Katie can go home today."

"What?" Carolyn asked in disbelief.

"When the doctors were making their rounds this morning they examined Katie," the nurse explained. "They found she is remarkably healed and ready to go home."

Rob and Carolyn walked into Katie's room and found her smiling. The intravenous tubes were gone. The pain-reliever drip was no longer taped to her little hand. It was obvious that the little girl no longer had pain. In twenty minutes they were checked out of the hospital and headed home.

Rob knows that the healing came from God. But what about the message that Katie would be going home the next day? When Sly spoke those words, no human had reason to believe it would be possible. The doctors and nurses all were agreed on a much longer time of healing. It wasn't until seven o'clock the next morning that the doctors knew that she had been healed.

And what about the messenger, Sly? "I have no doubt that he was an angel," Rob Kress says. What did he do? "The only thing he did was bring me good news. Katie Lynn is so little and so innocent, yet so radiant. We still have some bumps in the road ahead of us, but I'm positive that everything will be well. Thank You, Lord, and thank you, Sly."

JACKIE'S ANGEL

ROBERT STRAND

Jackie is a beautiful girl of seventeen with shining black hair and sparkling brown eyes. A delightful glow sets her apart from other beautiful young girls.

Three years ago Jackie faced a painful tragedy. Doctors had discovered a tumor on her cheekbone . . . the kind of tumor usually found only on a long bone such as an arm or leg. It had spread its deadly tentacles throughout the entire region of her face. Surgery offered the only hope to save Jackie's life. The doctors would be making an incision along the nose area and down through the upper lip. All of her teeth on the left side of her face would have to be removed as well as the cheekbone, the nose bone, and the jawbone. Needless to say, an operation of this immensity, performed on the face of a fourteen-year-old girl, was a grim prospect. Many tears were shed.

Several days before the surgery, lying in her hospital bed, she thought about what it would mean to go through life so terribly scarred, if indeed she even lived through the operation. She was frightened, for she desperately wanted to live. She wanted to experience all that life held for her. As she tossed on her pillow in lonely fear that night, she began to pray. With tears of anxious apprehension, she asked God to help her.

About two o'clock in the morning Jackie was awakened. She didn't know what woke her up, she only knew she was awake and alert. She saw a glowing light at the foot of her bed, and the silvery form of an angel appeared. The presence was very powerful and totally loving. An aura of stillness filled Jackie like the warmth of a summer day. She felt enfolded by the presence and a sense of incredible wonder touched every part of her body.

A voice filled with sunshine said, "Do not be afraid, Jackie. You are going to be all right." And then the angel presence was gone.

The following day, Jackie was taken to the X-ray room for preoperative X-rays. To the utter astonishment of the doctors, every trace of the tumor and its deadly tentacles was gone!

That was three years ago. Now here she is, this beautiful daffodil princess. Her face is unmarred, and she remains very much aware of God's miraculous touch upon her life!

COMPANION THROUGH THE STORM

JOAN WESTER ANDERSON

It was 2:00 P.M. on a weekday in April 1974 in Louisville, Kentucky. Lynne Coates and her husband Glynn were enjoying an unexpected break from work, sitting on the steps of their porch. Their older sons were soon due home from school. Their youngest child, Collyn, would be at kindergarten at Southern Baptist Theological Seminary until about five.

The couple chatted comfortably for a while. Although the early-spring day was calm, small thin lines of clouds rippled across the sky.

Glynn frowned. "Look at the sky. The last time I saw one like that was when I was twelve, when a tornado hit."

Louisville is part of the Midwest's Tornado Alley, and the weather service routinely issues tornado warnings or watches, especially in spring. "I think we had all gotten a little blasé about tornadoes," Lynne admits now. "I certainly didn't expect to see one."

But she did. The sky got darker, the wind picked up and Lynne began to feel apprehensive. The two older Coates boys came home, and as the tornado sirens began, Lynne made preparations to go into the basement. Glynn, however, hunted up his camera. "If I climb high enough," he told Lynne as he hoisted himself into the tree in their yard, "I ought to be able to get some great pictures."

"Are you crazy?" Lynne screamed at him over the rapidly rising wind. "I just heard on the radio that Brandenburg has been leveled. Get into the basement! It's really happening!"

The family huddled together underground, listening to the roar that sounded like a train bearing down on the house, and later, the pounding rain. Everyone's thoughts centered on Collyn. Was he safe? Why hadn't they gone earlier to pick him up? But who could have guessed that this time there would be a real tornado?

In just minutes the storm had passed and the family came out of the basement. Their neighborhood seemed relatively untouched, except for occasional debris and some downed power lines. "I'm going over to the seminary to get Collyn," Glynn announced, and left immediately. They would all feel better once their youngest child was with them.

Lynne gathered the older boys, and they gave thanks to God for bringing them through the storm. Then she found a portable radio and turned it on.

They listened to reports of the damage. And then they heard that the tornado had passed directly over the seminary. One of the buildings had lost its roof.

Oh, dear God, Collyn!" Lynne cried, and she flew to the telephone. She dialed the number of Collyn's kindergarten, but all she heard was the popping and crackling sounds that occur when a line is out of order. If the tornado had indeed gone in that direction, there must be a lot of damage, she realized. It was possible that telephone lines were down. But she had to know if Collyn was all right! And what was keeping Glynn? An ominous feeling settled within her heart. The seminary was only a fifteen-minute drive. Glynn should have been back before now.

Lynne couldn't have known that Glynn's route took him directly into the midst of the damage. What should have taken fifteen minutes would eventually take two hours, as he wended his way around uprooted trees, rescue vehicles, fallen wires, houses dumped helter-skelter and, perhaps worst of all, people wandering the streets in a daze. The storm had virtually destroyed a three-thousand-acre park of old trees next to the seminary, and Glynn had to park many blocks from Collyn's building. There was no way to drive through the devastation.

At home, Lynne tried again and again to phone the seminary kindergarten, but the number wouldn't ring. Instead, she would hear clicks, then the phone would fall silent. She grew more and more distraught, and both children began to cry. *God, I can't stand any more of this,* she prayed. *You're the only one who can help us now. Please watch over Collyn and the other children, and keep them safe.*

Once more, Lynne tried to phone. After a few clicks, the phone suddenly started to ring! A calm, pleasant-sounding woman then picked it up. "Don't worry," she said, answering Lynne's frantic questions. "The children are fine. They were all taken to another building before the storm. Their teachers will stay with them as long as it takes the parents to pick them up."

Lynne hung up, and she and the boys shouted for joy. Collyn was safe! They would just have to wait.

More than two hours later, Glynn and Collyn arrived. Glynn told Lynne that he had found a sign posted on Collyn's building door, telling parents where to go to collect their children. He went to the building and found Collyn there safe. Collyn had no memory of the tornado at all, except for noticing a bent weather vane on top of one of the buildings.

Lynne accompanied Collyn to his classroom on his first day back to school. She wanted to get the name of the woman who had relieved her fear on the telephone. "I'd like to thank her," she explained to Collyn's teacher.

The teacher looked at Lynne in bewilderment. "But you couldn't have spoken with anyone," she said.

"Oh, but I did," Lynne assured her. "You can ask my older boys. I was frantic until this woman assured me that Collyn was fine."

"Mrs. Coates, that would have been impossible," the teacher insisted. "We put a sign on the door, locked the building and moved the children before the tornado struck. There wasn't anyone here.

"And don't forget, our phone lines were destroyed. No call could have gotten through—or been answered."

Angels have been called our "companions in a storm." The Coates family knows, in a special way, what that lovely promise means.

ANGELIC EMPLOYMENT COUNSELOR

BRAD STEIGER AND SHERRY HANSEN STEIGER

No one can ever convince Mike Shapiro that it was not his prayers as a loving son that summoned the angel who found work for his unemployed artist father.

In 1972, when Mike was eight his father Benjamin, a talented artist-cartoonist, suddenly found himself out of a job. "Dad had drawn, inked and lettered for some of the top names in the syndicated comics," Mike said. "Although he had been a successful freelancer for many years, he had decided to take a regular job as a staff artist with a leading national publication when he found out that my sister Joyce was on the way. And now, just when he had placed all of his financial eggs in one basket, he was summarily fired."

Little Mike's hero was his father. The walls were papered with drawings, sketches and paintings that his dad had done for some of the biggest titles in the comics business.

"I wanted to be a cartoonist just like Dad," Mike said. "I would sit at my little desk and practice drawing in his style."

It was while he was at work late one Friday afternoon that Mike heard his father delivering the bad news to his mother.

"I can't believe it, Elaine," Dad said. "Just when we were getting used to receiving a weekly paycheck! Why did this have to happen now, with the baby on the way?"

His mom tried to console his dad with some words about their savings and the money that she got from her part-time job, but he wasn't accepting any comfort right then.

"You're not going to be able to work much longer before the baby comes, honey," Dad said. "And our meager savings won't hold out very long either. Let's just hope our money lasts long enough for me to reestablish my connections and start getting freelance work again. Otherwise, I just don't know what we're going to do."

The sound of fear and dismay in his father's voice greatly upset the eavesdropping eight-year-old. "Dad was always so upbeat and positive. It just broke my heart to hear him feeling so down and helpless."

Then Mike remembered how he had found himself recently drawing lots of pictures of angels. "I had really been getting into angels. There weren't a whole lot of books on angels back then, so I had asked our rabbi about heavenly beings. He told me about the angels that appeared to Abraham, the angels that had saved Daniel and his friends from the fiery furnace, the angel who had wrestled with Jacob, and so on.

My brain bubbled with all of these magnificent stories of angels and their obvious concern with us human beings.

"That's when I decided that I would ask an angel to help find Dad a new job. I remember that I must have prayed all night long."

It seemed strange to find Dad at home after school on Monday. Mom was still at work, so Dad suggested that he and Mike go for a walk.

Even to his youthful sense of direction and order, it seemed to Mike that his father was taking them on a rather erratic route. And when he spoke, his bits of conversation didn't make a whole lot of sense. Mike understood that his father was really troubled about being out of a job.

"We were in a neighborhood that was foreign to us," Mike recalled. "I knew that I had never been there before. But suddenly we were standing in front of this neat little restaurant, and Dad suggested that we go inside and order a sandwich and a soda."

Father and son had just received their sandwiches and sodas from a waitress, when a pleasantly smiling stranger, his hand already resting on the back of Mike's chair, asked if he might join them.

"I knew right away that he was my angel," Mike said. "He was well dressed in a blue suit, and he had light blond hair and bright blue eyes. He was a very attractive man with a pleasant, easygoing manner that made you feel good. And Dad, who was normally very reserved and aloof around strangers, just shrugged and said, 'Why not?'"

The man studied father and son for just a few moments and then said, "I'm sorry to learn about you being fired from your job, Benjamin. It is very difficult when such things occur in life, but you must not be discouraged."

"That cinched it for me," Mike said. "He had to be my angel. How could a total stranger in a strange neighborhood call Dad by name and know about him losing his job?"

Benjamin squinted at the man over the edge of his glass. "How do you know my name?" he wanted to know. "And how is it you know about my being fired?"

"Oh, I know a lot about you, Benjamin," the man said, giving Mike a knowing wink. "A great deal about you . . . and your family."

"You must work on the magazine," Benjamin said, believing that he had solved the mystery. After all, he had barely been employed there long enough to become adjusted to the working hours, to say nothing of meeting all the staff members.

The stranger smiled and denied working on the magazine from which Benjamin had just been fired. And then he proceeded to reveal just how much he really did know about the most intimate details of the life of Benjamin Shapiro. After a few minutes, Mike and his father sat mesmerized, their mouths hanging open.

"Then the most amazing thing of all happened," Mike said. "The angel told Dad where to go for a job. He gave him the address and told him whom to see.

"Next, he gave us both a little inspirational talk about always keeping our chins up and never becoming discouraged. About how we never really walk alone in life. That there's always someone to reach out a helping hand."

Both Mike and his father were so heartened by the man's message and the information about the new job that it took them a moment to realize that the stranger was no longer speaking to them. They looked over their shoulders to see that he was walking out the door.

"I've got to thank him!" Benjamin said, getting to his feet and tossing some money down for the sandwiches and sodas. "I've got to thank him for the tip about the job."

Mike remembered how the two of them ran after the stranger—but when they opened the restaurant door, he was nowhere in sight.

We had been right behind him," Mike said. "We opened the door only seconds after he did—but the stranger had vanished. Dad shook his head and speculated that the guy just blended right in with the people on the street."

Excited by the angel's appearance and disappearance and elated that his prayers had been answered, Mike told his father that the stranger was an angel. "I asked God to send us an angel—and He did!" he exclaimed. "I asked for an angel to help you find a new job—and he came!"

Benjamin laughed at his son's pronouncement. "He was one terrific guy, son, but he was no angel. You didn't see any wings or halo, did you? He was what you call a psychic, you know, a mind reader. But man, he was stupendous. I'll sure give him that."

That night at dinner, Benjamin told his wife about the incredible psychic that he and Mike had met on their walk. "This guy picked up on everything," he said. "He knew all of our birth dates, where we got married, our anniversary—everything. The guy was fantastic. He could be on stage, you know, like Dunninger or Kreskin or someone like that."

The next day, Benjamin followed through on the stranger's advice about the job opening. He went directly to the publication the man had recommended. He asked for the specific editor the stranger had suggested, and within the hour he was hired to begin illustrating the issue currently in production.

"Dad often remarked over the next three or four years how he would like to find 'that psychic' so he could thank him properly," Mike said. "I know that Dad went back to that little restaurant many times, thinking that the man might frequent the place. He described him to the manager, the waiters and waitresses, the cooks, the patrons of the restaurant, but no one claimed to recognize him at all.

"I know that the stranger was my angel, sent to us in answer to my prayers," Mike concluded. "No stranger, no matter how psychically gifted he might be, could have known so much about other human beings and have just the right job advice for my father. No, I know with all my heart and soul that the stranger was the angel that God sent to help Dad find work. And what is more, he winked at me."

ALL THROUGH THE NIGHT

LORETTA CASTEEN

Nicholas! I jolted awake and hurried to the bassinet at the foot of the bed where my infant son lay sleeping. I held my fingers inches from his mouth, desperate to feel the warmth of his breath. Relieved it was strong and regular, I crawled back into bed next to my husband Reno, knowing I would awake again to the same routine.

"Nicholas is a healthy boy," my doctor assured me. "You need to relax and get some sleep." I wished I could. While I was pregnant, I felt a sense of wonder and anticipation about what it would be like to be a mother. But when I held my son in my arms for the first time, I became consumed with worry. After a nurse came to talk to me about SIDS (sudden infant death syndrome), and the danger in letting the baby sleep on his stomach, that was all I could think about. If I didn't watch Nicholas every moment, I just knew something terrible would happen.

By the time Nicholas was three months old, my lack of sleep made me even more edgy. I spent most nights in a light doze, and I couldn't sleep while the baby napped during the day. When I closed my eyes I saw Nicholas lying lifeless in his crib, and I'd be wide awake again, terrified. My doctor's reassurances did little to set my mind at ease.

When Nicholas outgrew his bassinet, I insisted Reno set up a portable crib at the foot of our bed. One night we tucked Nicholas in, and talked for a long time. "You're not alone in this, Loretta," Reno said. "Nicholas is my child too."

Later in bed I told God how exhausted I was. *I can't go on like this. Please help me sleep so I can be a good mother to my son.* I shut my eyes and tried to ignore the horrifying images I saw. . . .

Nicholas! My eyes popped open. Propping myself up on my elbows, I prepared to throw back the covers—a movement at the foot of the bed caught my attention. *Who's there?* As my eyes adjusted to the darkness, I could just make out a figure beside the crib. A young girl. She was standing on her tiptoes, peeking down at Nicholas. Her curly hair was pulled back in a ponytail, with little wisps falling around her face. Was that lace on her pretty white dress? She seemed to be wearing petticoats, so that the skirt pushed out behind her as she leaned against the crib.

The girl turned slowly and looked at me, as if to make sure I was watching. She looked down at Nicholas once more, then walked toward the door. She reached for the knob, and faded away.

"Nicholas has a guardian angel," I told myself softly as I lay back and closed my eyes. He was my child and Reno's—and he was God's. For the first time ever, Nicholas and I slept until morning.

CHRISTMAS ANGEL OF HOPE

KELSEY TYLER

The story of hope was an integral part of Phyllis Scott's Christmas memories, and she would forever be touched when she shared it.

Back in 1911, when she was four and her brother was two, their parents, Jack and Martha, often struggled financially. Still, they shared an especially close bond and there was always enough food and love to go around.

That Christmas week was a troublesome one for the Scott family because Phyllis's little brother Tommy was sick; he had a high temperature and the doctors feared he might have polio. In those days, there were no vaccines for polio and many children died from that disease. Throughout the days and nights that preceded Christmas, Jack and Martha took turns kneeling by their sick little boy's bed and praying for his recovery.

In addition to the child's illness, there were other troubles that Christmas. The mill where Jack worked had cut his hours in recent weeks, and they had been unable to afford Christmas presents for the children. Martha had been secretly knitting socks and scarves, but her dream of buying Phyllis and Tommy each a toy and some candy had been shattered. Now it was all they could do to purchase food and other necessities.

The Scotts spent Christmas Eve gathered in Tommy's bedroom praying and singing carols and sponging the boy's feverish body. After a long and restless night, the Scotts finally fell exhausted into their own beds.

Very early on Christmas morning, when Martha was up fixing breakfast and arranging the wrapped parcels of socks and scarves by the children's plates, she heard a loud knocking sound. Martha tilted her head curiously and wiped her hands on her apron as she moved toward the front door.

"Yes," she said as she opened it.

There, on the front porch, was a handsome, well-dressed man and a pretty little girl. A large white dog stood at the child's side.

"Merry Christmas, Mrs. Scott," the stranger said in a soft voice filled with kindness. "I've come to see how Tommy is doing."

Martha stood staring at the man and child on her porch unable to comprehend how a stranger might know her name and the name of her child.

"Do I know you?"

The man ignored the question. "How is the child, Mrs. Scott?"

"Sir, who are you?" she asked. There was an unusual presence about the man; she was not afraid, but she wanted very much to know the identity of the stranger before her.

The man shook his head politely and smiled. "I came only to find out the condition of your son, ma'am," he said.

Still flustered, Martha ran her hand through her hair and took a deep breath and decided to answer the man. "Well, he's only a little boy, two years old," she began.

The man nodded kindly and the little girl beside him smiled. Martha continued.

"He's always been in good health until about a week ago when he caught this fever and—" she paused and her voice cracked. "Doctor says it might be polio."

"I know," the man said softly, reaching out toward Martha and squeezing her hand. "But he will recover shortly."

Tears began streaming down Martha's face, which she wiped away quickly. "Please, sir," she said, her face contorted in confusion. "Come in out of the cold and tell me who you are, how you know our names."

Again the man smiled and shook his head. "We must be going now," he said. "Close the door quickly so the cold doesn't get to the boy's room."

"But wait . . ."

The man waved once. Then he and the child and the big, white dog turned around and walked down the porch steps. Although he had cautioned her to close the door, Martha stood on the porch watching the trio to see where they were headed. Just as they reached the last step, Jack called out from the back room and

Martha turned away. When she looked toward the porch again, the man, the little girl and the dog had disappeared.

Martha ran quickly down the porch steps and scanned the street in both directions, but the sidewalks were empty. Dazed by what had happened, she walked slowly back into the house and shared the story with her husband.

"Who could he have possibly been?" she asked him.

"I don't know, Martha," Jack said. Then he smiled. "Maybe he was sent by God. A Christmas present to assure us that little Tommy is going to be all right."

The couple pondered this and, before waking the children, they prayed again for their sick son.

"I'm going to check on Tommy," Martha said as she stood up from the table. "You get Phyllis and tell her to come downstairs for a Christmas breakfast."

A few minutes later, when Jack was in Phyllis's room waking the girl and wishing her a Merry Christmas, he heard Martha.

"Jack, come quickly," she shouted.

Jack grabbed Phyllis's hand and the two ran down the hallway toward Tommy's room.

"What is it?" Jack was frightened; perhaps Tommy had grown worse or perhaps he had not have survived the night.

When they entered the little boy's room, Jack saw Martha sitting on the bed, her eyes glistening with unshed tears as Tommy sat grinning in her arms. She reached for her husband's hand.

"Jack, the fever's gone. He seems completely better," she whispered.

"Dear God," Jack whispered, and slowly, he knelt on the floor beside the child's bed. The Scott family held hands and thanked God for healing Tommy.

"And thank You, too, God for the stranger this morning. Thank You for giving us hope."

They did not see or hear from the strange man again until three years later, in April 1914. This time he was alone, but when Martha answered the door, she knew instantly that this was the same man who had visited them that Christmas morning.

"You've come again!" Martha said, opening the door and waving an arm toward her living room. "Please come in. I want to know your name, who you are."

But just as before, the man smiled and shook his head. "I wanted to tell you I'm sorry that your husband lost his job. But he will be working again soon."

This time, before Martha could say another word, the man smiled warmly, tipped his hat politely and turned quickly to leave. Martha called after him and watched as he turned around the corner of the house and headed toward the thick woods in back of their home. Martha ran down the steps after him, but by the time she got to the back of the house, there was no one in sight and not a sound from anywhere. Again, the man had disappeared.

Shocked by this sudden visit, Martha returned to the house and convinced herself that she must have been imagining things. The man must have been a different person, and he must have had the wrong house. After all, Jack had not lost his job. She silently thanked God that her husband did, in fact, have a job, and tried to forget about the stranger at the door.

That night, Jack came home from work earlier than usual with his shoulders slumped in defeat. He pulled Martha slowly into a tight hug and then sat her down gently on their worn sofa.

"I have some bad news," he said, looking deeply into her eyes. "I was laid off today."

Martha felt her heart skip a beat at her husband's words. The stranger had been right after all. She sighed deeply and told Jack about the visit from the stranger earlier that day.

"He said you'd be back working again soon," she said as she finished the story. "Jack, who is he?"

Jack shook his head in awe. "Whoever he is, he seems to want to bring us hope. Remember that Christmas morning when we wondered if Tommy was going to make it? He already knew everything was going to be all right and wanted to give us the same peace of mind. Maybe it's true. Maybe we have nothing to worry about now, either."

Martha nodded. "Well, let's go eat dinner. At least for now we still have food on the table." She moved to take off her apron, then suddenly she gasped.

"Jack!" she screamed. "Look!"

In her hand, she held a twenty-dollar bill, which had been nestled in her apron pocket. "Twenty dollars, Jack! Where in the world did it come from?"

For a moment Jack and Martha were silent, and then, at the same time, both reached the same conclusion.

"The stranger?" Martha asked quietly. Jack nodded and took her hand.

"Maybe he was more than a stranger, Martha. Maybe he was our guardian angel. It's possible, isn't it?"

For days, the couple pondered the stranger and his message. Then, two weeks later, Jack's job was restored, and he was given a bonus check for returning to the position. After that, the Scotts were convinced that whoever the man was, he was neither human nor ordinary. He had known their names and their needs, and he had brought them hope in times of despair.

Each year until Martha died, her faith remained strong as she told the story of the stranger who came bearing hope. The Christmas angel, she liked to call him.

In many ways, the stranger is still spreading hope today, as the story, which now belongs to Phyllis, continues to be passed down among the children, grandchildren and great-grandchildren of Jack and Martha Scott.

Chapter 2
God Sends His Angels with Provision

Elijah was afraid and ran for his life. When he came to Beersheba in Judah, he left his servant there, while he himself went a day's journey into the desert. He came to a broom tree, sat down under it and prayed that he might die. "I have had enough, LORD," he said. "Take my life; I am no better than my ancestors." Then he lay down under the tree and fell asleep.

All at once an angel touched him and said, "Get up and eat." He looked around, and there by his head was a cake of bread baked over hot coals, and a jar of water. He ate and drank and then lay down again.

The angel of the LORD came back a second time and touched him and said, "Get up and eat, for the journey is too much for you." So he got up and ate and drank. Strengthened by that food, he traveled forty days and forty nights until he reached Horeb, the mountain of God. There he went into a cave and spent the night (1 Kings 19:3-9).

Food and water and sleep. Our needs don't get more basic than that, do they? If we're deprived of any one of these things, our whole world becomes skewed so that we focus our attention on finding a way to meet that one fundamental need. When Elijah found himself at the end of his rope under a broom tree, he was fleeing from the wicked Queen Jezebel, having just trounced the priests of Baal (Jezebel's god of choice) in a showdown of sacrifices. God sent an angel to feed him. But this angel didn't just feed him, this angel cooked for him—warm cakes of bread served with fresh water. And not once, but twice, each time rousing Elijah from a restorative sleep.

God did not send an angel simply to point out the food Elijah could find for himself in the desert. This angel baked bread and served it to Elijah. Sometimes God provides for our needs simply by revealing the blessings that are available to us. But other times, He sends His angels to cook for us, to take the flour and water, form the cakes and bake the bread. And then to serve us, as the ministering spirits they are.

These stories reveal God's great compassion as He sent his angels to provide for us.

Fear the LORD, you his saints,
for those who fear him lack nothing.
The lions may grow weak and hungry,
but those who seek the LORD lack no good thing.

—Psalm 34:9-10

THE DELIVERY ANGEL

ROBERT STRAND

My growing-up years were wonderful and idyllic—a really happy childhood, as I look back. It never dawned on me that life was tough at times. My parents at that time were struggling to establish a mission church in the town of Evansville, Minnesota, which had a population of about eight hundred and fifty people, not counting dogs and cats. It was not easy. Dad had to work where he could find a job to support his family . . . it was just him and Mom, my brother one and a half years my junior, and me. We had a little garden and ate well when some of the church farm families brought goodies to the parsonage. I thought everybody had to live like that. The memories of those years are good. It's amazing what time can do to memory.

One particular night, however, is still a vivid memory. Mom set the table for herself and her two sons. One of us asked, "What are we going to eat tonight?" We looked around: the stove was cold, nothing was on the table except water in the glasses, nothing in the refrigerator, nothing in the cupboards. Not even a potato for watery soup. Not a cup of flour with which to make biscuits. Not even noodles for a hot dish of any kind. The house was bare and two boys were famished!

She said, "Let's sit down and ask the Lord to bless the meal." We dutifully bowed our heads and listened to her prayer.

"Dear Lord, we thank You because You are so good to us. Bless Dad tonight as he's away working. And, Lord, thank You for the food we are about to partake of, in Jesus' name I pray . . ." Before she got the final "Amen" said, both of us heard a noise on the back porch. We shoved our chairs back and in one motion ran for the back door, which was about six steps from the kitchen table and flung it open. There, sitting on the porch, were boxes of groceries! We ran out onto the porch and looked in every direction up and down that little dirt street in that little country town where everybody knew everybody and everybody knew everybody else's business. There was nobody! No car, nothing!

With great excitement we hauled the groceries inside and helped Mom put them away until they overflowed the cupboards and the refrigerator! Then we sat down to a glorious feast! We asked, "Mom, who do you think brought the groceries?"

She looked back with a smile and simply said, "Let's just thank the Lord for providing!"

WARM BLANKETS AND CHRISTMAS MONEY FROM AN ANGEL

BRAD STEIGER AND SHERRY HANSEN STEIGER

Merrie Riggs and Julie Wilkins believe firmly that the benevolent stranger who brought them blankets and money when they were young girls in North Dakota was an angel.

It was in November 1964. They were the Oltersdorf sisters then. Julie was fourteen and Merrie was ten.

"We were living in an old farmhouse that seemed to have more cracks than Daddy could patch with tar paper," Julie remembered. "We had lost our farm the year before, and we lost Mama to typhoid fever that summer.

"There were four of us kids—Steve, twelve, and Karl, eight, besides us two girls—who had to snuggle next to the old oil burner in the front room and try to keep warm enough to do our homework at night."

It was just after Thanksgiving when Merrie came down with a terrible fever. The kids had but one blanket apiece, but they all piled the covers on Merrie when they were doing their homework. Normally, they walked around the old farmhouse with blankets wrapped around them to ward off the cold, but they wanted Merrie to get warm enough to break her fever.

Since late October, their father, Gus, had been working at the grain elevator in town. During planting and harvest, he had been a hired man for Miles Hanson, but the elderly farmer did not need help during the winter months. The Oltersdorf family, however, still needed food, regardless of the season, so Gus worked at the elevator.

Julie remembered that their father was really depressed. It would be their second Christmas without the farm—and their first Christmas without Mama.

"We used to have really nice Christmases," she said. "We were never rich, but we were well enough off until Daddy had that run of bad luck. But, of course, more than our nice home and the presents, we would miss Mama terribly."

All the children noticed the deep melancholy that had possessed their father, so Merrie did not want to concern him with her illness. She knew that he had enough on his mind with the bills and all.

"I lay and prayed for one solid day while the other kids were at school," Merrie said. "I prayed that we could have some more blankets and just a little extra money so that we could have a nicer Christmas and so Daddy would not have to work so hard."

Merrie was lying next to the oil burner that afternoon when she saw her angel. She knew that her fever was getting higher, and she wanted Julie. Julie was the oldest and, just like Mama, always seemed to know what to do.

Merrie was startled to hear the door open, for she knew that Julie had locked it when she and the boys left for school that morning. Merrie was even more surprised when she turned to see a "beautiful" man walk into the house.

"He was fairly tall, well built, and I will always remember his long blond hair and his bright blue eyes," Merrie said. "I started to say something about trespassing, but he smiled and lifted a hand in a friendly way that seemed to say 'I won't hurt you.'

"He had four thick blankets under his arm, and he set them down on the kitchen table. For the first time I noticed that he wore hardly anything at all against the terrible November cold. He wore no coat, just a thin white shirt and blue jeans. I knew that he meant to give us those blankets, so I spoke up and said: 'You had better keep those for yourself, mister. You'll freeze to death in this cold climate.'

"I've always thought it interesting," Merrie said, "that young as I was, just ten going on eleven, I somehow felt that he had come from some warmer place. That was why I said 'climate.'"

The stranger smiled again and spoke for the first time, in a voice that sounded as if he were singing and talking at the same time. "I won't need the blankets. They are for you."

Just before the blond stranger left, he took five twenty-dollar bills from inside his shirt and set them on top of the blankets. "You'll be better soon, Merrie," he said as he walked out the front door.

After he had gone, Merrie was convinced that she had seen an angel. "I just knew that the stranger was the angel that I had prayed for to come and help us," she said. "And I will believe that until the day I die. And then I know that I will see him again."

Julie resumed her account of the incident: "When we got home from school, we found the front door locked just as we left, so we were really surprised when Merrie told us that someone had walked in on her that afternoon. And when she said that an *angel* had brought us kids each a new blanket and some money for Daddy, I felt her brow and got really scared. Her fever felt so hot. We covered her with those new blankets—wherever they had come from—and poured steaming hot tea down her throat until the fever broke.

"Daddy always felt that some nice young man in town or on one of the neighboring farms had learned of our plight and had given us the blankets and the money," Julie said. "One hundred dollars might not seem like much today, but in 1964 it was just enough to give Daddy the buffer he needed to get caught up with some bills, and he was even able to afford some Christmas presents for us.

"We kids always believed Merrie," Julie stated. "Even then she was a good artist, and she was able to draw a really good picture of the benevolent stranger. We had lived in that community all our lives, and we lived there another eight years—and none of us ever saw anyone who looked the way he did.

"I agree with my sister that an angel helped us survive that terrible winter of sixty-four."

CIRCLED IN RED

DOLORES BROM

P*lease, don't let him sit next to me.* I'd been job hunting for nearly a month, finding nothing but doors closed in my face, and now, after the worst Monday I'd ever known, this homeless man was probably going to sit beside me at the bus stop. I crossed off the last of the classified ads I'd pursued from Sunday's Austin *American-Statesman* and dropped the paper in the trash can.

"What kind of work are you looking for?" Sure enough, the man had sat down next to me. I ignored him.

I'd grown to hate waiting at bus stops. Many jobs I had applied for required reliable transportation and a city bus didn't qualify. Other jobs were too far off the bus route and I didn't feel safe walking home alone at night. I couldn't afford a cab, and buying a car was out of the question. I wanted work, but I constantly asked God for the perfect situation. *Is there any such thing?* I wondered.

"Finding a job is hard these days," the man said. "Sometimes life ain't fair. My mama used to say that, and you remind me of her."

I couldn't help looking at him this time. His clothes were wrinkled and worn, but under his shaggy beard he had a kind, gentle face. He was just down on his luck, as I was, and I felt for him. "I don't know how I'll ever find work," I began saying, and before I knew it, I was talking nonstop.

When the bus came the man pulled a folded newspaper from his pocket and handed it to me. "These folks are looking for someone just like you," he said. On the page was an ad circled in red.

I grabbed the paper and climbed on the bus, expecting the man to board behind me. I sat down thinking it was time I heard his story, but he wasn't there, and through the window I saw he wasn't at the stop, either.

"What happened to the man who was sitting beside me on the bench?" I asked the driver.

"There was no one there," he answered.

"But he gave me this," I said, waving the newspaper. The driver looked at me strangely, so I kept quiet.

I called the number in the ad the next morning, went for an interview and was offered the job the following day! The company had indeed been looking for someone like me. The job paid well, and it was on a bus route close to home. In fact, I've now been employed there for more than eleven years.

My prayers were answered by a scruffy old man who gave me Monday's edition of the *American-Statesman*. I'd never bothered to buy the Monday paper; all the ads ran on Sunday. All the ads, that is, except the one for my perfect job.

GIVE AWAY WHAT YOU HAVE?

QUIN SHERRER

What do you do when the pantry is empty? You might learn a lesson from Polly and David Simpchen—who needed a miracle.

David and Polly were expecting their first baby within the week, and times were particularly hard. David had been working, spraying ceilings for a small drywall company. He had not had any work that week, however, and the two of them were living hand to mouth. For the first time in their short married life, their food supply was down to nothing. They had no milk, no bread, no peanut butter. In the refrigerator was just enough hamburger to make one patty. The cupboard contained a can of vegetable soup, a little flour and a bit of sugar—all they had left.

That Sunday morning David prayed to God to provide money for rent, food and gas. Then they went to church, grateful they would at least be eating lunch with friends. In the afternoon as Polly was resting, she heard a knock at the door. She answered, seeing an unusually tall gray-haired woman. "I am hungry," she said. That was all—no further explanations.

"Come in and I will fix you a hamburger and some soup," Polly volunteered eagerly. She had never had such a request, but she wasn't going to let anyone go hungry!

"No, just give me the hamburger meat," the woman said. "I'll wait here."

Polly went to the refrigerator, ready to relinquish her last bit of meat. She silently prayed again her husband's prayer—that God would supply their needs. In faith that her prayer would be answered, she handed the woman the tiny portion of ground meat, all she had. The mysterious woman thanked her, turned and left. Polly called David quickly to tell him what had happened. They both looked out the window, expecting to see her walking down the sidewalk.

But she was gone. They ran out into the yard. Polly went to the left, David to the right. They looked everywhere for her. But she had disappeared. They were puzzled.

The next morning on their front porch they found an envelope with a check and a note from some neighbors. It was enough to cover their rent, some food and gas for the car.

Polly saw a glimpse of God's graceful plan that is often beyond our imaginations. He had given her the gift of faith to believe He would take care of their needs, even if she gave away their last portion of meat to a stranger. And He had honored her generosity.

MANNA IN THE WILDERNESS

ROBERTA MESSNER

Like hundreds of thousands of other nostalgia seekers, my dad's favorite Labor Day weekend event was the huge flea market in Hillsville, Virginia. For fifteen years he'd packed up his treasures and rehearsed his music and tales and headed south, from Huntington, West Virginia, down to the Blue Ridge Mountains.

His destination? A twelve-acre weed field overrun with trucks and vans and jalopies jammed so close they were locked in for four days. From tailgates and tables, over six hundred vendors from all over the country traded their collectibles and told their stories. Dad's specialty? Violins. Come evening, a strip of grass at one end of the midway became a bandstand, where my dad and his buddies fiddled away the night.

But in the summer of 1989, Dad was diagnosed with cancer. By the first of September he was in the middle of heavy-duty radiation therapy. The seven-mile ride to the local hospital and back home each morning wiped him out for the entire day.

Living just a few miles from my folks, I stopped in nearly every evening after I got off work at the hospital where I was a registered nurse. The week before Labor Day weekend, I pulled Mom aside on the porch. While Dad dozed in his living room recliner, I whispered, "I don't see how he can possibly go to Hillsville this year, especially with the scorching weather they're predicting. Look how weak and short-winded he is. And that's here in the house, where he sits in his recliner all day. If he gets sick in Virginia, it's going to be one big mess. Once you've parked on that midway, there's no getting out. You're locked in. What would he do?"

"Honey, I wish he'd reconsider, too. But you know your dad. Once he's got his mind made up, there's no changing it," Mom said. "He's looked forward to this trip all year long."

Still, Mom, my younger sister Rebekkah and I reasoned and cajoled and begged Dad to cancel his trip.

No. He was going. And he convinced his doctor to postpone a Friday radiation treatment—on one condition, that someone go with him.

Afraid that he'd pack his precious violins into his van, hop in and head south alone despite the doctor's orders, Rebekkah and I quickly juggled our work schedules and got the weekend off. With health problems of her own, Mom wasn't up to making the trip. We reserved a motel room near Hillsville, close enough to keep an eye on Dad without pestering him. I packed a satchel full of his prescriptions and other potions that might relieve distress. There was the pink stuff, the chalky stuff, fizz-fizz tablets . . . and Mom packed a cooler full of Dad's favorite sandwiches, salads and snack foods.

Propelled by sheer willpower, Dad got up before dawn on Friday and packed his van for the three-hour trip south to Hillsville.

"Now you be sure and eat to keep your strength up," Mom instructed, kissing Dad good-bye. "And sip on one of those cold Seven-Ups when you're out in the sun." As Mom hugged Rebekkah and me, she added, "You all just go and have a good time—and don't worry. I'm trusting God to take care of things while your dad's so far from home. It will all work out. You'll see."

Then she handed us two big, brown empty shopping bags. "Can't wait to see what you come home with," she added, the porch light burning in the background. That was Mom—always expecting an empty bag to be filled to overflowing with blessings.

Rebekkah and I followed in my Oldsmobile, discussing contingency plans, what we were going to do with Dad if—or when—the trip got the best of him. We also whiled away the hours imagining what finds we'd buy. Years before I'd been to the Hillsville market with my husband Mark, looking for vintage household decorations and parts for his old truck. Now I had a more serious interest in antiques. In addition to my nursing career, I was a part-time photo stylist for several country-style decorating publications. I hoped to uncover some great photo props. And Rebekkah was always trying to add milk bottles and Shirley Temple memorabilia to her collections.

While Dad found his spot in the market morass—turf he'd earned by squatter's rights—we parked along the side of the road and walked twenty minutes to the entrance gate.

Once inside the gate, we quickly tracked down Dad and helped him drag his folding table, green canvas umbrella and violin cases from the van. "You girls go ahead and mill around and let me do this," Dad insisted, beads of perspiration forming on his forehead. "I'm not an invalid yet."

We sat on a patch of grass and talked to the vendor next to Dad about the costume rings he was selling. "I'll keep a close eye on your father," he promised when Dad wasn't listening. "He's really gone downhill since last year."

About that time a squirmy kid wearing coveralls and a red bandanna moseyed up to the table with his mother to check out Dad's fiddles. "You play the violin, young man?" Dad asked.

The boy, maybe eight, nodded sheepishly.

"I was about your age when I tried my hand at it, son. Learned on a two-dollar model from Sears and Roebuck. Back on the farm we didn't have much to entertain us except music. Pick one of these out and play me a tune." Dad tapped his feet as the kid squeaked "Little Brown Jug." "Why, you'll be fiddling 'Soldier's Joy' before you know it," Dad said through a strained smile, steadying himself on the edge of the teetering metal table.

To hunt up the restrooms, Rebekkah and I left Dad, decked out in a big straw farmer's hat and sagging in his folding chair. We swung back by his table to give him some advice on the contents of the medicine satchel. "If you get the least bit nauseated in this heat," I cautioned, "be sure and take a dose of that Maalox."

"Maybe you better take a couple of Tylenols now, just in case," Rebekkah piped up. "Here's a bit of Mom's good ol' potato salad to chase them down with."

Dad obliged. "Okay, mother hens, did you crack your car windows? Be sure and put some sunblock on your face and arms, and get yourselves something cold to drink every little bit. Where's your hats? There's no shade in this place...."

We laughed and left to comb the aisles, searching for any old, red-handled kitchen utensils or Shirley Temple collectibles. We frequently checked in on Dad, then we'd wander off, through the wilderness of discards, until worry got the best of us again. Then we'd swing back around. Each time he looked fine, though he wasn't shooting the breeze with potential customers.

After we'd eaten a corn dog and fries for lunch, Rebekkah fixed Dad a sandwich, which he turned down. The guy parked next to Dad pulled me aside.

"I think you should know that your dad hasn't eaten a bite all day," he said in a confidential whisper. "He sits with his head in his hands until he spots you two coming. Then he tries to pretend like nothing's wrong."

I went back to chat with Dad and asked him about a tin pail at his feet. "In case I get sick to my stomach," he explained.

The nurse in me couldn't pretend any longer. "Dad, if you don't eat a little something, you're going to get even weaker. Isn't there *something* you'd try to eat?"

"There is one thing I keep thinking about," he answered. "An old-time country dinner—the salt-side ham we used to eat on the farm. There's nothing like that around here, I'm sure."

"I haven't seen any, but you never know," I said. "We'll go ask and see what we can find."

"Who can figure that?" I said as Rebekkah and I headed to the nearest concession stand. "As sick as he is, and he wants some home-cured Virginia ham."

We found hot dogs, hush puppies and funnel cakes, but nothing resembling Dad's request.

Returning to give him a report, we passed a vendor displaying white wicker furniture. For sale at the next booth was a big-ticket dining room suite with chairs decorated with carved lions' heads. The next man was peddling turquoise and red feedsacks that said Dixieland. I snatched one up as a birthday gift for my friend Dixie.

And next to him a long table covered with rainbow-hued glassware strangely beckoned us under a green and white striped canopy. As we admired the hodgepodge of dishes and knickknacks, a woman with white, wispy hair wearing a blue calico apron spoke to us. "You girls hang around a minute," she instructed before disappearing inside a camper.

Seconds later, she opened the door and walked down the steps carrying a paper plate heaped with food and a tall Styrofoam cup of iced tea. "Virginia-baked ham for your dad," she explained handing me the plate.

Rebekkah and I stared at each other. Rebekkah stifled a giggle behind her hand. "I can't believe it," I said under my breath, spying Dad's favorite fluffy lemon meringue pie for dessert.

The grandmotherly woman explained, "I added a pinch of pepper to the potatoes and black-eyed peas. Sure hope he gets to feeling better." For a brief moment the shade under the striped canopy was as cozy as a farmhouse kitchen, a pull-up-your-chair kind of place.

Rebekkah interrupted my reverie. "Oh, boy, iced tea! Could I get one with Sweet'n'Low and no lemon?" she asked.

The woman shook her head and planted her hands in her apron pockets.

"This is the kindest thing that's ever happened to me at a flea market," I said.

"You know, I work for a few magazines. I should write a story about this. People need to know about folks like you."

An angelic smile crossed the lady's face. "You do that," she said. "You just do that."

Like excited schoolgirls, we rushed across the aisles to Dad's table to present him with our find. "*Psst.* Wait till we get home, and I tell Mom she's got a little competition here," Rebekkah kidded, giddy with delight.

"Dad, your friend up the way sent you this," I explained. "A small lady about your age. White hair. She has eyes that look right inside your heart. I guess we didn't get her name."

He perked up and accepted the gifts. "Don't know anybody by that description," he said as he sipped his tea. "Say, since when did you learn to sweeten my tea just the way I like it?"

"The woman did it, not me."

"Well, run back and find out who she is. And thank her for all this." He sank his teeth into a slice of warm ham.

Dutiful daughters, Rebekkah and I retraced our steps, crossing through several aisles to find the canopy. There, next to the Dixieland feedsack dealer, we saw not the green and white canopy but an unfamiliar brown pickup truck. A man, dressed in a T-shirt and cut-off jeans, was selling old lamps. We talked to the feedsack dealer. How could the canopy and camper have fled the scene so quickly? And where was the elderly lady?

"Been here all day," he said. "Haven't seen anyone like that. And that truck pulled in here same time I did this morning. You girls sure you know what you're talking about?"

Rebekkah hummed the theme from *The Twilight Zone* as we noodled along back to Dad.

As we got close to his van, we both noticed that he wasn't there. *Now what?* I thought, expecting the worst.

But his neighbor next door grinned as he gave his report. "Your dad just sailed his empty paper plate into that trash can and took off to do some Christmas shopping. Asked me to watch his table for him. Says he's planning on playing his fiddle after the sun goes down."

We started laughing. "I'd like to know what was in that food," Rebekkah said. "That lady was nowhere to be found when we went back to thank her. Everyone we asked about her looked at us as if we had completely lost touch with reality."

Dad's neighbor stared into the distance as if he was contemplating the universe. "Manna from heaven, that's what I think. It's right in the Bible, you know. The hungry Israelites were wandering in the wilderness, wishing they were back home in Egypt. Then food dropped right from the sky."

We stayed at Dad's table until he came back, which wasn't for about an hour. We hovered over him. "Dad, how you doing? Here, have a seat. Here, take a drink."

But he was smiling and joking and hardly winded, like his old self. But not exactly. The old Dad would never have held out his hand and placed in my palm a gift he'd bought himself, a women's gold, Victorian, pocket-style watch to wear on a gold chain.

"What's gotten into him?" Rebekkah whispered as Dad tidied up his table, whistling an old mountain tune.

He turned to Rebekkah. "And I tried to find you a Shirley Temple doll. This isn't the year, honey. Nobody had a thing.

"Now, you girls can go home now. No need to baby-sit any longer. I'm doing good enough to be here on my own."

We were not convinced, so the next day we drove two hours south to check out another flea market. When we returned, Dad convinced us to drive on home. And he took care of himself the rest of the weekend.

When Dad pulled into the driveway Monday evening, he was still whistling. The rest of the weekend had gone well, with no need for our well-meaning potions and contingency plans. Just as Mom had predicted, God took care of everything.

A ministering spirit. As time passed, Rebekkah and I had no other explanation for the calico woman we couldn't track down. Hadn't God fed Elijah by sending ravens? And, yes, for forty years God provided the Israelites with manna that appeared every morning like dew on the grass. Surely He was capable of sending an elderly woman with a plateful of Virginia ham, as unlikely as a supernatural, ministering presence seemed in that swampland turned flea market.

THE GROCERY LIST

BETTY MALZ

I t is too easy to rush ahead of God and bring on all sorts of difficulties. We must wait for His leading, then act obediently.

One couple who did exactly this—and who were delivered by angelic material provision—were Mr. and Mrs. Kenneth Ware, Americans living in Paris during World War II.

The Wares were horrified to hear that Jews were being taken from their homes, loaded like cattle onto trains and transported to camps where they faced death in the gas ovens. The Wares could not have known that six million Jews would eventually lose their lives in these camps, but they believed God was leading them to help as many as they could. So they began the perilous task of secretly hiding Jews, feeding them, praying with them and helping them escape under the cover of darkness to countries where they would be safe.

Food was rationed so strictly that at one point the Wares had no supplies left in the house and no means of replenishing their empty cupboards. They had spent what money they had, and buying on credit was impossible. Besides, they did not want to draw attention to themselves with the quantity of food they needed.

Believing God could still meet their needs, they decided to write out a shopping list in the form of a prayer. Mrs. Ware got out paper and pencil and made a list of everything she needed: meat, apples, carrots, her preferred brand of flour and many other supplies. Then the Wares knelt together to pray.

A knock at the door brought them both to their feet.

"Who is it?" called out Mr. Ware.

"Please let me in," responded a soft, urgent voice.

Thinking someone must be in need, Mr. Ware opened the door and was surprised to see a tall man dressed in white.

"I have the items your wife ordered," he said, setting two bags down on the table.

"But there must be some mistake," responded Mr. Ware, shutting the door. He looked in wonder at his wife, who was removing from the bags every item she had written on her prayer list. Everything was there, down to the brand of flour she had specified.

When they both looked up to thank the man, they realized, to their astonishment—though only seconds had passed and the door remained closed—he was gone. The stranger had left even more mysteriously than he had appeared.

Rejoicing, the Wares knew that an angel of the Lord had brought their provisions. No one else had known their needs, or would even have had those specific supplies on hand. It also taught them—and me—that angels can provide the most practical kinds of assistance for those to whom they have been sent by God, in response to godly prayer.

ENTERTAINING THE STRANGER

ROBERT STRAND

I t happened in a southern state. Eugene and Judy had eight kids ranging in age from five to fifteen. They were a churchgoing, loving family. Gene had worked at a local lumber mill for years, and when it folded he was left with doing odd jobs for a living. One day he had a small job in town working on a car. Judy on that day was doing the laundry when some church ladies dropped over for a visit.

Their conversation was broken when Judy's oldest child came into the house, "Mom, there's a man coming around to the back door. Says he's got to talk to you."

Immediately the church ladies warned, "Be careful. Don't have anything to do with a man who's comin' begging! Now hear!"

At the back door stood the elderly black man with graying hair and soft, warm eyes. "Ma'am, sorry to bother you, but my truck broke down and I'm walking to town. I would appreciate it if you could give me some water and just a bit of food if you could spare it."

Judy was stunned . . . she found herself hesitant to do the right thing. She had been influenced by the ladies. Instead of getting the water and food she stood there. Eyes met, and the old man waited a few seconds and then silently turned away. Judy felt ashamed as she went back to the table, but worse was the condemning look from her oldest son.

Quickly she grabbed a pitcher of lemonade and some cookies and ran out the front door to find the old man on his knees with the children around him listening as he was telling them a Bible story. She offered the cookies and lemonade and told him to wait as she went back to prepare a sack lunch. She returned, "I'm sorry about the way I acted."

"That's all right . . . too many people are influenced by others. But unlike some, you have overcome it and this speaks well for you."

That night, Gene had wonderful news. The car he had repaired belonged to a man whose brother ran a repair garage and was looking for a mechanic. He hired Gene on the spot!

Later, Judy told Gene about the events of the afternoon. When she finished, he asked, "Did you say this was an elderly black man? Kind-looking eyes and gray hair?" He jumped out of bed and went through his pockets until he found a piece of folded paper, which he handed to Judy, saying, "I met that man walking down the road when I came from town. He waved me over and gave this to me. When I finished reading it, I looked up and he was gone, just disappeared!"

Judy began to cry as she read the note: *Do not forget to entertain strangers, for by so doing some people have entertained angels without knowing it.*

SWING LOW . . .

WILLIAM D. WEBBER AND MARILYNN CARLSON WEBBER

I t's the little foxes that spoil the grapes, the Old Testament writer reminds us. Little things can make our lives crazy. For Helen Shirling, it was a hammock.

At Christmas, Helen and her husband had always put their tree on their glassed-in front porch where it could be seen from the street as well as from the living room. To make room for the tree, they always moved the hammock from the porch to the basement.

Helen's husband had died the previous May, so this year he was not there to help. Taking the hammock apart had always been easy. With one person on each end, a quick tug was all that was needed to pull it apart. Tackling the job by herself was quite a different matter. Helen tried to push and pull at the same time, but the old hammock refused to budge. The grandchildren and the neighbor children had played hard on the hammock, and the frame seemed stuck for good.

Not really, Helen thought. *If I call my son, he would be glad to help me.* But Helen wanted to show that she could do for herself.

Helen tells the story: "I knew I should wait for my son to help me, but I wanted it done right now. You've heard the saying, 'Lord, grant me patience, but

I want it right now.' We have a large basement, and when I couldn't budge the hammock, I thought I could just leave it together and drag it downstairs.

"I dragged the thing through the house, knocking things down as I went. When I got to the basement door, I found there was no way I could turn it around to go through the door and down the stairs. I was perspiring and disgusted with myself for not waiting for help that my son would have so willingly given me.

"I thought of Billy Graham's saying that we have personal angels. I cried out, 'If there are angels all around me, why don't they help me when I need it?'

"Right before my eyes that hammock fell apart. Pieces rolled across the floor and under the table. All I had to do was pick up the parts and carry them to the basement.

"I froze in my tracks when it happened. To this day I still get goose bumps when I tell about it."

For Helen, it's good proof that angels help even when we don't deserve their assistance. She is still amazed that the angels were not so high-and-mighty that they weren't above taking a hammock apart.

"The family has never let me forget it, and they laugh about Helen's angels. Now whenever they see an angel figure in a store, they buy it for me."

Helen has a nice angel collection. "How did you get so many?" friends ask.

"It's a funny story," Helen replies.

Chapter 3
God Sends His Angels with His Message of Healing

Send from the heavens Raphael thine archangel, health-bringer blessed,
aiding every sufferer, that, in thy service, he may wisely guide us, healing and blessing.
—St. Rabanus Maurus

There is probably nothing that renders us more vulnerable than illness or injury, whether it's our own sickness or that of someone we love. Our bodies become weak and defenseless, our emotions exposed, and our faith in God's care and goodness wobbles in the face of pain and hopelessness.

It is at our points of greatest helplessness, when we are most vulnerable and at risk, that God sends His angels to bring us word of God's healing touch. Angels assure us that healing is available from God, and in so doing, they restore our hope—which of course is no small part of healing.

Early in the book that bears his name, Isaiah records an encounter with God in which he sees God in all His holiness and glory, attended by seraphs—angels with multiple wings who surround God, singing His praises and calling to one another, "Holy, holy, holy is the LORD Almighty; the earth is full of his glory." The Temple trembles from their thundering voices and smoke fills the air. And Isaiah was completely undone, totally aware of his incompleteness and unworthiness in the presence of a Most Holy God. One of the seraphs lifts a live coal from the altar and flies to Isaiah, touching the coal to his lips, declaring him to be whole and without sin.

At first, healing may seem to involve only our physical bodies, but in truth, healing is about restoring us to wholeness: physically, emotionally, mentally, spiritually. And that means we must be open to the healing that God offers to us in every area of our lives. As with Isaiah, it may be that an angel is the agent of God's healing. And, of course, the angels always point us back to God.

These stories show us God's healing work through His angels.

> Praise the LORD, O my soul,
> and forget not all his benefits—
> who forgives all your sins
> and heals all your diseases. . . .
> Praise the LORD, you his angels,
> you mighty ones who do his bidding,
> who obey his word.
> Praise the LORD, all his heavenly hosts
> you his servants who do his will.
> Praise the LORD, all his works
> everywhere in his dominion.
> Praise the LORD O my soul.
>
> —Psalm 103:2-3, 20-22

JENNIFER'S HEALING ANGEL

BETTY MALZ

When little Jennifer Rose was born, her parents, Phil and Mavis Church, were filled with joy and gratitude to God for entrusting them with a new little life. But their happiness soon took on an edge of fear. When she was just two days old, the doctor detected a certain abnormality in her physical responses. He ordered tests immediately, and stunned the parents by reporting "positive" results: mental retardation was likely, in addition to a number of possible physical disorders.

Test followed test in order to diagnose Jennifer's condition, and by the time she was four months old, having spent much of her short life in the hospital, her little body was sore from the probing needles. She also showed a fear of strangers.

Phil and Mavis Church clung to their belief that Jesus conquered pain and sickness by His death on the cross. But a temptation began to seep into their thoughts and conversation: the temptation to doubt that God could heal this little child, and even that He was caring properly for her. It was especially difficult to keep hoping in God's care when each day seemed to bring more symptoms and more devastating news.

At six months Jennifer was tested for cerebral palsy; then she began having violent seizures. After weeks of praying and hanging onto the thinning threads of hope, Phil and Mavis checked Jennifer into another medical center for days of specialized testing, thinking their situation could hardly get much worse.

But it did. Doctors broke the news to them one Saturday morning, when the Churches had left their two older daughters with a sitter all day, that Jennifer had a tumor on her brain that had to be removed immediately. The operation itself was risky, but without it she would certainly die. They had little choice but to consent to the operation. Surgery was scheduled for the following Tuesday morning.

Then, in what seemed an unusual move, the doctors agreed to let the parents take Jennifer home for the weekend, so the whole family could be together. "But be careful," warned one of the doctors. "One blow on the head could possibly end her life."

Heavy-hearted, Phil and Mavis barely spoke during the few hours it took to drive home. Once there, they settled Jennifer into her crib, where her two sisters cooed to her through the bars. Then the tired and concerned parents went into their bedroom and dropped to their knees together in prayer. The temptation to doubt that Jesus would or could heal Jennifer was almost overwhelming. But once more, resolutely, they offered themselves and their child to His care.

As they continued to pray, they heard a knock at the door. Mavis got up to answer it, while Phil started to head into Jennifer's room to check on the girls. But through the glass storm door they both saw an unshaven old man in tattered clothes standing on the porch.

They exchanged glances. This was a stranger, after all, and how could they handle anyone else's problem right now? But sympathy for the sad look on the old man's face must have won out, because Mavis opened the door.

"Could I have something to eat please?" he asked. "If you could give me something, I'll sweep your porch for you."

Mavis glanced at Phil, then nodded. Phil joined the old man out on the porch while Mavis went to the kitchen to fix some food. The conversation soon turned to the foremost subject on Phil's mind—Jennifer's illness. As Mavis came out and placed a tray with a sandwich and cold drink on the small porch table, Phil was explaining about the tumor and the operation their little one faced on Tuesday.

The old man's eyes filled with tears, the food seemingly forgotten. "May I see her?" he asked.

Phil hesitated. Besides, Jennifer was afraid of strangers. But something in the man's appeal caused Phil to nod and lead the way to the crib.

Jennifer was still the object of her two older sisters' doting attention, but as soon as she saw the old man she smiled and reached out her hands to him. Phil started to speak, to tell the man not to lift her for fear the child's head would be bumped, but for some unknown reason he kept quiet. The old man leaned down and lifted Jennifer up, gently cradling her and talking to her softly. Then he put a wrinkled hand on her head and said, "Little angel, you will not have to have surgery, for there is no longer anything wrong with you." Then he smiled at Jennifer and put a nickel into her tiny fist.

He handed the child to her father, turned and walked out the door.

For a moment the young parents stared at each other. Then they heard the storm door swing shut. Mavis hurried to the door and looked out. There was no sign of the man, and the sandwich remained untouched where she had put it on the table.

That night they all marveled over how peacefully Jennifer slept, and the contentment she showed all day Sunday. Only on Monday morning did Phil and Mavis feel the familiar stabs of fear, the temptation to despair.

They made the long drive to the medical center, entrusted Jennifer to the doctors and awaited the results of the final examination and X-ray prior to surgery the following day, almost afraid to breathe.

They did not have to wait long. Soon two doctors appeared, shaking their heads and looking puzzled. "We can't explain it," said one, "but the X-rays show no sign of the tumor."

"We don't know what happened," added the second doctor, "but we would like to keep her here for a couple of days just to make sure she's all right."

In the days that followed, the doctors affirmed their new findings. They handed Jennifer once more to her parents, but this time with a smile and assurances that "she's fine."

That ride home was a celebration. Joy swelled in the their hearts as Phil and Mavis each thanked God for fulfilling His promises and remaining true to His Word. And that night before they tucked each of their three healthy children into bed, Phil opened his Bible and read aloud: "Let brotherly love continue. Be not forgetful to entertain strangers: for thereby some have entertained angels unawares" (Hebrews 13:1-2, KJV).

THE GRAY LADY

JOAN WESTER ANDERSON

Angelic rescues are sometimes dramatic. But they can also come softly, in such a tender manner that the one being helped is unaware of the supernatural aspect until some time has passed. Jean Doktor of Oceanside, California, knows this very well.

In 1980, Jean's husband John was struck by a strange illness. He had been a healthy sixty-year-old, jogging every day, but after returning from a business trip he ran a mild fever, which soon soared to one hundred and five degrees. John's physician prescribed antibiotics, but by the next day the fever had not broken and John was acting strangely. "Whenever I spoke to John, I seemed to hear two voices in his response," Jean recalls. One was the familiar tones of her husband, now vague and wandering. Seemingly under that voice, however, was another, this one deep and comforting, which to Jean seemed to be saying, "You will get through this, John."

Jean called the doctor again, reporting not only the symptoms but the two-voiced phenomenon. "He must be hallucinating because of the high fever," the doctor told Jean. "Get him to the hospital right away."

Jean did, and although the diagnosis was pneumonia, John soon rallied and was sent home. But the strange symptoms reappeared, and by the time John had been rushed again to the hospital, he had fallen into a semiconscious state. "The doctor told us that John could hear our voices, but could not respond to us. Instead, he would repeat every word we said to him," Jean says. "It was a nightmare. My healthy reliable husband was failing right in front of me."

During the next few days, John faded in and out of awareness. Four specialists entered the case. They took spinal taps and blood cultures, even checked the possibility of chemical poisoning, but remained baffled. Nothing seemed to work—and there was nothing more to do.

By Saturday night, the Doktors' three grown children had gathered in their father's room, shocked at his deteriorating condition. Jean wept quietly with fear and exhaustion. It seemed obvious that John was slipping away from them, and she could do nothing at all to help. "Please God," she prayed, as she held his limp and unresponsive hand, "let me keep my husband. I need him . . . I love him. . . ."

On Sunday morning, Jean was alone in the room, watching John's drawn and pallid face. There was a knock, and she rose to face an elderly lady dressed stylishly in gray silk, her white hair beautifully arranged. She was carrying a little gold container holding communion hosts, and Jean assumed she was what Catholics term a "lay minister," someone who brings the Eucharist to hospital patients.

"Get Brother John on his feet," the woman told Jean in a firm but friendly tone.

Brother John? Who was this person? Jean was sure that a lay minister would never interfere with a patient's routine. "That's impossible," she protested. "My husband can't move."

"He needs to stand up," the gray lady repeated in a gentle but reproving tone. Jean was irritated at the woman's high-handedness. What if the floor nurse came in and found them disturbing John? Yet Jean also felt compelled to obey this brisk but oddly reassuring stranger, so much so that she suddenly reached for her husband and pulled him to a sitting position. The woman looked on, composed and quiet.

John was groggy, but he didn't protest Jean's efforts, and somehow, with her support, the two of them stood swaying. Then the gray lady gripped both their hands, and waves of cold electricity shot through Jean.

"We earnestly request the healing of Brother John," the gray lady murmured, "and may the love of Jesus touch him. May he be instantly healed."

She placed the wafer on John's tongue, snapped the little gold box shut, turned and briskly left the room. Jean helped John into bed, where he immediately fell into a deep sleep.

That had been an odd episode, Jean mused. She was fortunate that hospital personnel hadn't caught her dragging John out of bed! But it had been nice of the nurse to break the visiting rules. Grateful, Jean popped her head out the door. "Thanks for allowing John to have communion," she told the nurse sitting at the desk. "The lay minister just left."

The nurse looked at her. "I've been sitting here for the last twenty-five minutes," she replied. "I didn't see anyone leave your room."

Puzzled, Jean approached a woman at the door of the next room. "Did you see anyone coming out of our doorway?"

"No." The visitor shook her head. "And I've been standing here for at least a half hour."

Jean checked all the rooms on the floor, then went to the waiting rooms and reception hall. The gray lady had not registered at the desk. There *had* been a group of Catholic men bringing communion to the patients, but no woman of any age or description was among them. Exasperated, Jean gave up. It was peculiar, but best forgotten, especially since John seemed to suffer no ill effects.

John slept all day, and at 4:30 that afternoon he abruptly sat up in bed. Jean went cold with apprehension. Was he hallucinating again? But no. "Are the kids waiting in the foyer?" he asked her.

"Yes. Would you like me to get them?"

"No. I'll get dressed and walk down to visit with them."

"Absolutely not!" Jean gasped. "You're terribly sick. You'll be even worse after all that exertion—"

"I feel just fine, honestly," he told her.

Jean looked closer. John's waxen complexion had turned rosy; he looked better than he had in weeks. Relenting, she helped him into slippers and robe. The look of relief and joy on the children's faces when they saw him confirmed Jean's own suspicions. Her husband was going to get well.

The doctor examined John thoroughly the following morning and was completely mystified. "John's fever is gone, his eyes are clear and he might as well go home as there isn't a sign of illness," he told them. "I simply can't explain it." Jean saw no reason to mention the gray lady, not to a doctor of medicine. But John returned to normal activity within two weeks, and he has remained healthy to this day.

For a long time, Jean resisted the idea that their mysterious visitor had been an angel. Didn't angels appear in white shining robes, wearing gold halos? By contrast, her gray lady had been efficient, no-nonsense, detached and completely in control of the situation. "She commanded firmly, prayed firmly and, after finishing her mission, vanished firmly," Jean says. "She was the most unangelic spirit I could ever imagine."

And yet . . . who could doubt the wondrous healing that had occurred? And hadn't there been comforting signs all along the way, evidence that she and John were not alone in this ordeal . . . hadn't she even heard that "second voice" reassuring her? "I think many people experience these special touches," Jean says, "but we're afraid others will ridicule us if we talk about them. But I was there, I saw the change in John, and now I consider life a loving gift."

Nor will Jean forget the fervent prayer she whispered during the crisis of illness. "Please, God, let him live . . . I need him . . . I love him . . . send me a miracle . . . ."

God did—and a messenger to bring it.

THE ANGEL CAME ON WEDNESDAY

ANN CANNADY

Until that incredible morning, I thought that angels were something you saw on Christmas cards or read about in the Bible. I never conceived of them as beings who could step into our lives.

Seventeen years ago my life was in terrible turmoil. At forty-four, I had recently been diagnosed with uterine cancer. I agonized over the possibility that I might leave my four children motherless. My husband Gary, a strapping former Air Force master sergeant, was devastated. He had lost his first wife to the same type of cancer. He took me in his arms and with tears streaming down his face said, "I can't bear the thought of losing you."

My doctor scheduled a radical hysterectomy for later in the month at Cape Fear Valley Hospital. Meanwhile, Gary and I did the only thing we could—we prayed. Every day we knelt together and asked God to heal me, to give us time to raise our children. Friends and fellow members of the Haymount United Methodist Church also prayed for me. We had everyone we knew praying. But as the surgery date loomed, I felt my faith begin to waver. What lay ahead seemed so frightening. I knew God was a healer, but I didn't know anyone who had ever been healed.

It was the Wednesday before I was to enter the hospital. Gary and I got up and ate breakfast. Again we prayed together.

At about ten o'clock, as Gary was doing some chores around the house and I worked on bills at my desk in the solarium in our front foyer, the doorbell rang. Gary answered it. When he opened the door I heard a deep, melodious voice say, "I've come to tell Ann."

I turned to see a tall black man standing on the doorstep. He was taller than my six-foot-five-inch husband. His skin was ebony and his eyes were a deep, shimmering azure. He looked past Gary and fixed his gaze directly on me. "Ann," he said, "the cancer in your body has been healed."

"How do you know?" I managed to gasp.

"God told me," he answered.

I stared at him uncomprehendingly. I noticed his unusual clothing. He wore a loose, black, gossamer tunic with swirling golden threads, and dark, flowing trousers. His shoes were woven from some ribbonlike material. He was clean-shaven with close-cropped hair, and there was an aura of peace about him.

"Would you like to come in?" I said. I glanced at Gary, who was as awestruck as I. He stepped aside for the man to enter.

"Sir," I said, standing up, "I don't understand. . . . What is your name?"

He smiled radiantly and touched his left shoulder with the index and middle finger of his right hand. "My name is Thomas."

Speaking in the most comforting tones, Thomas told me I must not worry. He quoted Isaiah, "And with his stripes we are healed." And then he said, "Before I go, I must pray for you."

He held out his right palm about twelve inches from my forehead. "Father God," he began, and as he prayed I felt intense heat radiating from his hand. My legs weakened, my eyes closed and as I fell gently to the floor I was aware of a powerful white light moving up through my body.

I awoke to see Gary leaning over me. "Ann, are you all right?"

"Where is he?" I asked. But Thomas had vanished.

I crawled to the phone and called my doctor. "Something has happened to me that I can't explain," I said. "I won't need the surgery."

The doctor said he realized how the stress and fear could be affecting my imagination. But I insisted. Finally we compromised. If I would show up for the surgery, he would perform another biopsy as I lay on the operating table before any further procedures were done.

I agreed. And that Sunday I entered the hospital as planned. When I awoke in my room afterward, my doctor was at my bedside shaking his head. "Ann, I can't explain it. Your tissue appears clean. We didn't operate. We'll do further tests, but for now you're in the clear."

In the years since, there has been no recurrence of the cancer. Thomas did not return. But no longer do I think of angels as confined to Christmas cards. I know that they are here among us, doing God's work in our lives.

THE MAN IN THE CORDUROY JACKET

CHAD JOHNSTON

All in all, I consider myself a normal fifteen-year-old. I play football and piano. I'm into computer games. But a lot of people, especially Mom, Dad and Grandma, say I am a miracle. I guess I can't argue with that because even though it's been a long time, I still remember the day the miracle happened, the day I met the Man.

I was only four years old when my mom and dad took me to St. Jude Children's Research Hospital in Memphis, Tennessee, to find out why I was so sick. I had to have lots of tests, including one that hurt so bad I couldn't imagine why I was being put through it. I remember seeing other kids in the waiting room—some bald and bloated, some with plastic bags on their laps in case they threw up. One boy had had his leg amputated. I remember thinking, I hope that doesn't happen to me.

Dr. Rochelle Nuss performed the most painful test. She held a huge syringe down by her side and away from me. I think she didn't want me to see it, but I focused on it right away; it reminded me of a meat thermometer, and it scared the heck out of me. "Chad, we need your spine to be curved for this procedure," she said, positioning me on the examination table. "It's going to hurt a little, but just relax and it will be over before you know it." That last part was true. It only took about thirty seconds to draw out the marrow and fluid that needed to be tested, but it was the longest thirty seconds of my life. It was scary to feel the cold metal all the way up inside my back. I wailed and begged Dr. Nuss to stop. "Just a couple more seconds," she whispered.

Mom was on her knees in front of me, holding my face, telling me it was almost over. We were both crying. Finally Dr. Nuss pulled out the needle and said I had been very brave. Then I had to lie still with a pillow under my rear end for about an hour.

I knew they were testing for something called leukemia, a form of cancer. After the test, I got worried. Mom and I watched TV in the room. I remember it was the day the *Challenger* exploded, and we saw all the sad faces at Cape Canaveral. Several hours later a nurse told my mother that the doctors needed to see her. When Mom came back a little while later, she took my hands in hers and squeezed real tight. "Chad, honey," she said, "you do have leukemia. I'm sorry, but I truly believe you are going to come through this just fine." Then she hugged me hard. Cancer seemed unreal to me. It was something that happened to adults. I couldn't imagine being so sick I might die. Kids weren't supposed to die.

I had to stay in St. Jude that first week after the diagnosis so I could start chemotherapy right away. Leukemia weakens your immune system because it affects your white blood cells, and chemo can really throw your system for a loop; so for my own protection I was put in a room by myself. Only one visitor was allowed to sit with me at a time. I could see it was a big deal. Everyone had to scrub before coming in, and visits were limited. Separated by a big glass window was a room where Mom and Dad stayed and kept an eye on me. We talked back and forth on an intercom.

On the day the Man appeared in my room I was feeling awfully bad from the chemo. The IV needle in my hand hurt. I was really scared about what was happening, and I had asked God why it was happening to me.

Grandma sat in a rocker next to my bed while Mom looked on from the parents' room. Mom hardly ever took her eyes off me all that week. She was like a mama bear looking after one of her cubs. She saw the Man as soon as he appeared in my room. So did Grandma. *Maybe he's the hospital chaplain*, I thought. He kind of looked like a preacher, but I didn't see a badge or anything. He wore a tan brushed-corduroy jacket. I looked through the glass at Mom and she seemed surprised too. How did he get in? Why hadn't the nurses stopped him? I already had one visitor. Grandma and I glanced at each other. I knew she was thinking what I was thinking, but neither of us could manage to say a word. It was strange. As Mom would say, the cat had definitely got our tongues. Finally the Man spoke.

"A friend of yours sent me," he said in a low, soothing, reassuring voice. Somehow we knew not to ask which friend. We just knew to stay still.

"My name is Dan," he continued, very matter-of-fact but friendly. He moved to the side of the bed. "Chad, I am here to pray for you." Then the Man pulled back my covers and put his hands on me. Mom, Grandma and I just looked at one another. "I'm going to lay my hands right here and I'm going to pray for your healing. Is that all right?"

I wasn't scared at all. Excited, maybe, but not frightened. I nodded my head. "Sure," I said in a whisper. Slowly, gently, he rubbed his hands back and forth across my belly. As he rubbed he spoke the sweetest, most indescribable prayer. It was like words and music all in one beautiful sound. I didn't understand it, yet I knew it was good, that it came from God through the Man. I felt a warmth all through me that was awesome. Mom said later that my eyes got huge.

I don't know how much time passed. When he was through, the Man smoothed out the covers and tucked the blanket under my chin. He smiled, leaned over and said, "Chad, you are going to be just fine." He turned, looked at my grandmother and sort of nodded to Mom through the window. Then he walked out of the room.

We couldn't move or speak; it was as if we were frozen. We just stared at one another. After a minute Grandma jumped from her chair and hurried to look out the door. She peered past the double glass doors, where people entered the hallway, clear to the open elevator on the other side of another set of doors. No sign of the Man. The long hallway was empty. When Grandma questioned the nurses, they all shook their heads and replied, "What man? We didn't see anyone." The Man had just walked in and walked out without being noticed. That seemed impossible.

What was real, though, was the definite fact that I suddenly felt a whole lot better. I wasn't so sick and the pain was almost gone. Instead, there was a warmth where the pain had been. I sensed right away that the Man had done more than simply pray for me.

A week later, after the initial chemotherapy was over, we moved to a motel down the street so I could have the rest of the treatment on an outpatient basis. I was feeling pretty weak. When Mom tucked me into bed, I curled up under the sheets and asked, "Mommy, could you lay your hands on my belly and pray for me like the Man did?"

"Sure, Chad, I'll try," Mom answered. She put her hands on my stomach and said a nice prayer. But when she finished I sighed. It was different. "Mommy," I said, "you can't put warm into me. Your hands, they're not hot like the Man's." I was afraid she might be mad at me. Instead, Mom and Grandma just laughed and laughed. I hadn't heard them laugh like that in a long time, and I joined in.

Fifteen days after the Man's visit, Dr. Dow, my outpatient doctor, told us that the chemotherapy had chomped up all but a few leukemia cells. (Dr. Nuss had explained that chemo was like Pac-Man. It would chomp up all the bad cells.) Twenty-one days later, after the rest of the initial chemotherapy treatments, the cancer was gone.

As I said, I'm fifteen years old now and I live a normal life with no hint of the disease. Doctors don't like to use the word *cured*. They say my leukemia is in remission. The word my family and I like to use is *miracle* because, for us, it was nothing short of that. I still remember as clear as yesterday how sick I was. And if I close my eyes and concentrate, I can feel the healing warmth from the hands of the Man who visited me that day when I was four.

A LIFESAVING BABY'S FORMULA FROM AN ANGEL

BRAD STEIGER AND SHERRY HANSEN STEIGER

When Craig Green of Binghamton, New York, was six months old, he was slowly dying because he could not retain any food. Because of some malady, which the doctors in 1933 were unable to diagnose, he weighed less than he had at birth. Although the Green family physician and other medical experts had spent long hours with the infant, they were unable to determine either the cause or the remedy for baby Craig's rapidly deteriorating condition.

One night Sarah Green, Craig's sorrowing mother, looked toward a window in the bedroom and saw an angel robed in white coming through the screen.

"Be not afraid," the angel said in a gentle voice. "I have come to help you. Your baby is dying, but if you heed what I tell you, he will soon be well."

As the astonished mother listened, the supernatural visitor advised her to prepare the baby's formula according to his directions. "Make the formula of whole milk," the angel prescribed. "Add a little cream and beat an egg into the milk. Your baby will be able to keep this down."

The heavenly being walked to where the child lay sleeping. "Behold your son," the angel said, smiling. "He sleeps peacefully."

Tears coursed down Sarah's cheeks. "But the doctors say that little Craig will soon sleep in death," she said, barely managing to force the words past her sorrow.

The angel turned to her and spoke to her in a stern, authoritative manner: "Cease your weeping. Your boy will live to be a fine man.

"Now you will lie down," the angel seemed to add as a secondary command. "You will sleep long and peacefully. Good-bye."

Before the young mother's startled eyes, the angel floated through the screened window and disappeared.

When the doctor called the next day, Sarah decided not to tell him of her angelic visitation. But she did ask about the formula that the heavenly being had prescribed for her baby.

The doctor heard her out before he responded. "Well, under ordinary circumstances and conditions, I would feel that a change of diet might be harmful." Before he completed his reply, the doctor hesitated several seconds. "But I must be honest with you, Mrs. Green. Little Craig seems to be walking the road to death. You might as well try the new formula. You have nothing to lose."

Since Craig Green is now sixty years old, there remains no question that the angel-prescribed formula worked for him.

"Mother told me how she knelt in prayer to God and thanked Him for sending the angel to save her baby," Green told us. "The change in formula might well have been the sole cause of my survival, but I have often felt that there was much more to the angel's visitation than that. I am convinced that the angel also exerted a great deal of healing energy and that the change in formula may have been only incidental to my rapid recovery."

THE STEWARDESS

SAM CATHEY

In 1967, my first year in evangelism, I had to rush back from a revival to be with my family. My daughter had been hospitalized with acute appendicitis, possible rupture and possible peritonitis. They were trying to get her temperature down so they could operate in the morning. I got on a plane in Los Angeles about 2:30 in the morning. I was heading to our home in Detroit. My heart was very heavy. Because it was my first year in evangelism I was insecure, unsure about what I was doing except that I knew it was God's will. I didn't want to be away from the family, didn't want to be out on the road as I was. And here trouble had come the first few months of my new venture for Christ. My seat was at the bulkhead, right behind the first class curtain. When we were airborne, a stewardess came by. She wore a red dress with blue trim.

I asked her, "Do you mind if I go up into the first class section, there's no one up there. I am going home and I need to rest. May I go up there and make a bed?"

She said, "No, I'm sorry. I can't let you go up there. It is against the rules. We don't even have a stewardess up there."

So I said, "Okay, I'll make it right here."

She had just walked away when another stewardess came through the curtains. This one was dressed in a blue uniform with red trim. She invited me to come up front and sit with her, and I gratefully agreed. We sat facing each other, and she asked if I'd like some refreshments. I thanked her and she brought me some sandwich squares, olives, chips and pop. I began to eat and she began to talk. She went on and on about the Lord, Scripture, the sovereignty of God's grace, about God's love, care and protection. I forgot I was hungry and sleepy and just listened.

Now mind you, not a word had been said about my daughter Nola, not one word. And I'd not identified myself in any way as a minister. After a good while, we passed over Chicago. She stood and said, "See all of those lights down there? Put your hands like so." She put my hands together and held them out there. "See, from way up here, it looks like you cover up the whole city of Chicago, doesn't it?" I agreed. "Now cup them so," and I cupped them. "From up here, it looks like you're got the whole city of Chicago in your hands, doesn't it?" Again, I agreed.

She then put her hand on my shoulder, looked me full in the face and said, "O thou man of God, Nola will be all right." With that statement, she wheeled around and went through the curtains into coach.

I was stunned. I'd not even mentioned Nola's name. A few seconds later, I got my composure and went after her. I couldn't find her, I ran into one of the other stewardesses and she asked where I'd been. I told her I'd been sitting in first class, and she said, "I told you that you couldn't go up there."

"Well, the head stewardess came and got me."

"I'm the head stewardess."

"No, I'm talking about the one dressed in blue with red trim."

"Oh no, we don't have anybody like that on this plane. You've been dreaming."

"No, she took me up there and gave me some sandwiches and things."

"Now I know you're dreaming. There's no food up there."

I said, "Let's go see." We went back up there and there was a remnant. This stunned her.

I described the woman, and the stewardess got the other women together, and they went from one end of that plane to the other, looking for the stewardess. We could not find her. So I told the stewardess what she had said about Nola, my daughter, and they were just stunned, as was I. We looked everywhere. And of course, she was not to be found.

When I got off the plane that morning, my wife picked me up just grinning from ear to ear, and said the hospital had just called, the fever had broken, the blood test was clear. No indication of any kind of infection, no pain or anything, not even a need for surgery. They told us to come and get her and take her home. We went by the hospital and took her home.

Years later, when my daughter was twenty-six and the wife of a Baptist pastor, she went into a hospital for surgery. After the operation, the doctor came out and said, "Mrs. Cathey, we can't find a surgical scar indicating that Nola had her appendix taken out." My wife said, "No, she never did have it taken out." The doctor looked at her and said, "Well, we thought while we were in there we would go ahead and clip that appendix. We found a surgical scar where the appendix was suppose to be, but there's no external surgical scar."

I know that's a wild, weird story, but it can be documented, at least most of it can be, especially the medical reports on my daughter. It is my earnest and honest conviction that God sent that angel to me to encourage me, not only about my daughter, but to give me faith in my new venture as an evangelist, a faith which would keep me on the road for twenty-two more years.

Chapter 4
God Sends His Angels to Guard Us

At that time the disciples came to Jesus and asked, "Who is the greatest in the kingdom of heaven?"

He called a little child and had him stand among them. And he said: "I tell you the truth, unless you change and become like little children, you will never enter the kingdom of heaven. Therefore, whoever humbles himself like this child is the greatest in the kingdom of heaven . . . .

"See that you do not look down on one of these little ones. For I tell you that their angels in heaven always see the face of my Father in heaven" (Matthew 18:1-4, 10).

When we think of angels, we usually think first of guardian angels, those angels who are sent by God to keep us safe when we're vulnerable or defenseless. A guardian angel will step in when we face danger (seen or unseen) or when we are unable to protect ourselves.

But most of us associate guardian angels with children, who are particularly susceptible to injury and danger. We know we're to provide safety and care for them, yet we recognize that the dangers that threaten children loom much larger than our powers to protect. Since children are considered more vulnerable and in need of heavenly protection, we never hesitate to ask God to provide that protection.

Jesus often uses children to illustrate the truths about God's relationship to His creation. People tend to discount children and their understanding of adult matters, such as finance, morality and, yes, spirituality. But Jesus didn't make that mistake. When asked about what life in God's realm is like, Jesus chose a child to demonstrate that in order to understand God we need to be like children. This led to other discussions of spiritual matters, but before moving on, Jesus returned to the child and warned his listeners: "See that you do not look down on one of these little ones. For I tell you that their angels in heaven always see the face of my Father in heaven." In other words, this child whom you discount has angels who have access to God Himself.

The stories that follow celebrate God's own emissaries who guard us all, children and adults alike.

For an angel of peace,
faithful guardian and guide
of our souls and our bodies,
we beseech thee, O Lord.

—Orthodox prayer

SUBWAY SENTINEL

EVELYN FEHLBERG

New York City can be exciting and scary all at once. In 1970 I was a freshman at a design school, getting to know the Big Apple. After commuting from my parents' home in Irvington, New Jersey, for a while, I'd found a tiny apartment in Greenwich Village.

One Sunday evening in January, I was waiting for the subway at West Forty-second Street. The station was deserted, and it made me uneasy. I was used to seeing the platform bustling with people. *It's the weather*, I thought, hugging myself against the freezing cold. *Where's that train?*

I glanced at the stairs, hoping another passenger would appear. Most of the time I wasn't afraid in the city. "There's no problem here," I would tell myself if I felt nervous in a crowd or walking alone on a dark street. "God is always with me." It usually worked. But not that night. That night was creepy.

Finally, I heard the rumbling and roaring of an arriving train. The loud noise sounded like music to me. The train doors slid open, and I stepped aboard with a sense of relief. But the subway car was empty too, and I felt anxious all over again. I chose a seat near the door. Only three stops to Greenwich Village.

A man entered my car at the next station. He stood looking around for a moment, and then as the doors closed took the spot right next to me. "God is forever on my side," I tried to tell myself.

The man sat calmly, staring straight ahead as the train began to move. He wore a knit hat pulled down over long, shaggy hair, and a scarf draped his shoulders. He wasn't a large man, but I was much smaller, and no match for him if he wanted to harm me. "You don't know this," he said quietly, "but I'm your guardian angel." *What should I do?* I thought frantically. *I'm trapped on the subway with a crazy man.*

Wham! The door between the cars slammed open. A gang of teenage boys stormed in, maybe nine of them, walking single file, shouting and cursing. They punched each other in some macho display, and kicked the seats as they swaggered down the aisle.

Trembling, I stared at my lap, clutching my purse. These guys were looking for trouble. The man sat silently beside me. When the gang passed in front of us, one of them said, "Aw, there's nobody in here!"

They left the train at the next stop, and the man patted my hand. I wasn't sure what to say when we both got off at the station in Greenwich Village. My guardian immediately blended into the crowd on the platform. But the One who sent him would forever be by my side.

AN ANGEL OF MY OWN

ROCCO FRANCISCO

When I was a small boy my family lived on the North Side of Chicago. My mama, my papa and my four siblings all lived together in a small apartment in the bustling heart of the city. It was kind of a tough neighborhood, but we kids enjoyed it—we ruled the streets with our games of kick the can and stickball.

Our lives followed a set pattern every day. First Papa would leave for work at the break of dawn, trying to tiptoe out of the little flat so as not to wake the rest of us. Once awake, the older kids, Mary, Tony and Joe, would busy themselves getting ready to take the trolley to school. I was too young for school then, so I had to stay home with Mama and the little baby. I didn't really stay home, of course. Most of the time I was outside the apartment building playing with the other kids my age, all too young to go to school but too old to want to stay inside with babies. And each afternoon I would leave my pals and run down to the corner where the trolley stopped. I'd be there waiting when Mary, Tony and Joe all piled off. I couldn't wait for the day when it would finally be my turn, too, to get on that old trolley and ride to school like a big kid.

But there was one warm and sunny Chicago day when my mother would not let me go outside to play. "Why not, Mama?" I pleaded. "I don't want to stay inside all day!"

"I'm not sure," she admitted. "Just a feeling I have. I want you to stay inside with me today," and all day long she kept me busy with small tasks, everything from shelling fava beans and peeling potatoes to rolling out biscotti dough—anything to keep me inside as long as the ominous feeling persisted within her.

At last the long indoor afternoon was ending. I could see from the clock that it was time for me to go down and meet the trolley. I put on my little cloth cap and jacket and reached for the door. "Rocco, no!" my mother shouted, running toward me. "I don't want you to meet your brothers and sister today. Instead I want you to . . . take a nap."

A nap? I was six years old! Why should I take a nap at my age? But she insisted, pulling off my hat and coat and ushering me into my bedroom. She watched from the doorway as I reluctantly climbed into bed and closed my eyes. Then she quietly shut the door and tiptoed away.

And then something incredible happened. As soon as I rested my head on my pillow a burst of white light filled the room, temporarily blinding me. When the spectacular light began to fade, I could see the most glorious angel at the foot of my bed. Every detail was clear—the angel appeared to have shining wings and was crowned with a golden halo. He hovered lightly in the air a few feet away from me, with his arms outstretched in a loving way. I felt a warmth spreading throughout my body, a feeling of pure love and complete security. It was not frightening; it was glorious. The vision lasted only a minute or two, but the intensity of that feeling has stayed with me my whole life. When the angel left my room I rested my head on my pillow once again, enveloped in a feeling of serenity and joy.

Not long after this incredible experience, I heard the sounds of my brothers and sister running up the wooden stairs. They burst into the apartment with great cries of excitement. "Mama, Mama!" they called out. "It was so exciting! You should have seen what happened. A trolley car slipped off its tracks and skidded into the corner telephone pole at Race Street. You know the corner, Mama, the corner where Rocco waits for us each day. It's lucky he wasn't there today, Mama!"

Mama said nothing, but her eyes welled with tears and she bent her head in silent prayer. I opened the door of my bedroom and whispered, "Mama, Mama, come here!" Wiping her eyes on the corner of her apron, she entered my room. "Right there, Mama. He was right there!" I pointed to the foot of my bed. "It was an angel that came. An angel of my own that came to protect me!" Abandoning herself to her emotions, Mama sank to her knees and put her arms around me. "Oh, Rocco, I didn't know what might happen today," she sobbed. "All I knew was that I needed to keep you near me, to keep you safe." And safe she had kept me, safe at home with my own magnificent guardian angel.

"GO HOME—NOW"

MYRLE E. DIENER

Before we moved to Davenport, Iowa, in 1973, my family had never lived in the Midwest, so we weren't used to the region's often violent weather. Two tornadoes touched down near us that spring, doing terrible damage. After the first one, my husband and I practiced survival techniques with our two children. When an electrical storm was forecast, we huddled together in the basement. Lesley, ten, was the most frightened, and she shivered in my arms until the danger passed. "Don't worry. Mom's here," I told her. I hated to think of her having to make it through a storm without me.

The May morning I met some friends at the Palmer Hills Golf Course there wasn't a cloud in the sky. We planned to play well into the afternoon, so I had told the children to let themselves in after school. Lesley would like being the grown-up, and I trusted her to look after nine-year-old Scott till I got back.

"Hurrah!" I shouted after I made my putt at the eighth hole, just one over par. This was my best score so far. "I'm on a roll," I said. I was waiting to tee up at the ninth hole when I noticed everything had become very still. The birds had stopped singing, and there wasn't a breath of wind. I looked around. The sky had turned dusty yellow, with big clouds fringed in charcoal.

"A storm's coming," I said, nervously checking my watch. The children ought to be getting home right about now.

"It'll blow over in a few minutes," one of the women reassured me. They were all longtime residents. *I guess they know best*, I decided. But when it was my turn at the tee I kept thinking of Lesley, probably more anxious than I was that it was another tornado. Distracted, I hooked the ball into a ravine about one hundred and fifty feet off to my left.

The others got in their carts and started across the fairway. I went to search for my ball. As I approached the ravine I saw a man. I stopped, afraid. He must have been eight or nine feet tall, by far the biggest man I'd ever seen. He was muscular and powerful-looking, dressed in a white tunic belted at the waist. His copper-colored skin shone—as if light came from inside him—and I realized who the imposing presence was. No wonder angels in the Bible announced themselves with the words "Fear not."

He looked straight at me and said, "Go home—now!" I didn't hesitate. Shouting good-bye to my friends, I jumped into my cart and raced to the clubhouse. I reached the parking lot as the first drops of rain began to fall and was soaked by the time I got to my car.

At home Scott met me at the door; Lesley was in the basement. She threw herself into my arms, tears pouring down as hard as the rain. "Oh, Mom, I was so afraid. I asked God to make you come home!"

It took Lesley a while to get over her fear of storms, but I didn't worry as much, knowing God and His angels are always with us, close enough to hear a child's desperate plea.

SWEET DREAMS

Betty Malz

Steve Doherty, who works for the Trinity Broadcasting Network, told me of the struggle he and his wife Theresa had once had getting their young son to sleep peacefully through the night. I was especially interested in this problem since I get letters and phone calls constantly from parents whose children between the ages of four and nine are afraid to go to sleep.

For two long years, every night from the time he was four, Ryan Doherty would cry at bedtime, beg to sleep with his parents and wake up several times in the night terrified from nightmares. Steve and Theresa tried everything. They played Christian music, read happy bedtime stories, reassured him, prayed with him—even spanked him. They counseled with a pediatrician and talked with a children's psychiatrist; and always, it seemed, they were told that they had done everything they could to assure Ryan he was safe and loved. They were completely baffled.

Finally an elderly gentleman in their church suggested they try two things. First, he said, when Ryan went to bed, they should have him say the name Jesus until he fell asleep. Second, they should read aloud a certain prayer in Ryan's room after he fell asleep each night; he wrote a copy out for them. It spoke of faith in the Word of God, and the safety Ryan had surrounding him as a child of God.

Steve and Theresa had prayed similar prayers before, with the exception, they noticed, of one line: "We believe and confess that You will give Your angels charge over Ryan and accompany and defend and preserve him in all his ways."

That night they followed their friend's suggestions, and awoke the next morning astonished that they had not once been disturbed by calls from Ryan in the night. Soon their son burst into their bedroom, all smiles.

"Ryan, you slept all night long!" Steve exclaimed.

"I sure did, Dad," he replied. "I wasn't afraid after that angel came."

Steve and Theresa exchanged glances. "What angel, honey?" asked Theresa.

"The one who was here last night. Didn't you see him?"

They shook their heads.

"Oh. Well, he walked down the hall and stopped at your door and looked at you, and then he came into my room. He stood by my bed, and slid his hand under my head. And do you know what he said?"

Again they shook their heads.

"He said, 'Ryan, don't you ever be afraid again.'"

"What did he look like?" asked Steve.

"Like Jesus," he answered without hesitation. "He wore a dress and there was a light with him. It looked like the dining room curtains when the sun comes through. He lit up my room."

From that night on, Ryan has slept peacefully, secure in the assurances of his visitor, and Steve and Theresa believe that an angel ministered to their son's needs.

MOTHER'S HELPERS
Teri Johnston

Many children have imaginary friends; child psychologists say it's a very normal part of their development. When my daughter Tiffani was three years old, she started talking to two imaginary friends that she called Chauncey and Tetet. They played all kinds of games and went everywhere together. I didn't think much of this—I thought it was kind of cute to hear her talk to her two playmates. But on July 10, 1996, a very unusual event occurred that proved to me what special friends these two actually were.

We woke up that morning to our regular routine of getting dressed and cleaning up the house. We played a few games together, and then I put Davis, my six-month-old son, down for a nap. At lunchtime, Tiffani helped me make sandwiches and chips, and then asked if we could have a picnic out on the balcony. It was such a beautiful day that I said it would be a wonderful idea. Out the door we went, carrying plates, cups and napkins, with Tiffani's doll tucked under my arm. We all sat down around the table—Tiffani, me, the doll and, of course, Chauncey and Tetet. We were having a lovely time chatting about the noisy blue jay that haunts our home with his loud chirping when I thought I heard Davis crying. I told Tiffani to be good while I checked on the baby, and that I would be right back. Her reply was "Don't worry, Mommy, my friends are here." I smiled at her, picked up our plates and went in the house.

I put the plates on the sink and looked in the crib, where Davis was still peacefully sleeping. It seemed that only a minute had passed when I heard a very unusual thud coming from the balcony area. I guess in my heart I knew what had happened, but I prayed I was wrong. I ran to the door and looked out. Tiffani was not on the balcony. My heart was pounding as I took the few steps across the patio and looked over the twenty-foot drop to see my little girl lying motionless on the dirt below.

I flew down the stairs to the basement, saying over and over, "Please, let my baby be alive, please!" As soon as I opened the back door, I heard a faint whimper, which sounded like heavenly music to my ears. I had just completed an emergency training course two weeks earlier (an inspiration, I believe), and so, instead of picking her up right away, I did a quick head-to-toe assessment, as the instructor had taught us to do. Upon finding all her bones intact and no complaint of any head, back or neck pain, I gently picked her up in my arms and just sat there crying. After a couple of minutes, we made our way into the house and up the stairs to the rocking chair.

Not wanting to let her go to sleep for fear of concussion, I cuddled and talked to her for a long time. After about twenty minutes, she started complaining that her stomach was hurting. My first thought was that it might be internal bleeding. I called the hospital and they instructed me to bring her right in. I alerted my husband and parents, packed up Tiffani and Davis and headed out on the longest fifteen-minute drive of my life. After the doctor examined and X-rayed her, he informed us that there was no discernible internal bleeding and that we should take her home and keep an eye on her.

Later that afternoon I allowed Tiffani to take a nap. She slept peacefully for a while but then woke up crying, complaining again about her stomach. She could stand up but couldn't bend forward. I called the hospital again, and they instructed me to take her to Primary Children's Hospital for a CAT scan and other tests. Once there, Tiffani remained quite calm until the moment they strapped her down to do the CAT scan. Then she started crying, begging me to help her. I stood there, trying to be strong but feeling so helpless; I thought my heart would break. I kept asking myself over and over, Why did I leave her? Why did she fall off the balcony? She had never done anything like that before; why now?

After I held Tiffani down for more blood tests, all the while reassuring her that things would be okay as she cried in my arms, she finally fell into a deep sleep. I looked over at my parents, who had been there to support me the whole time. Emotionally exhausted, I reached out to them and cried in their arms. My mother looked at me and said, "I know Tiffani is going to be all right. I don't know how to explain it, but I just feel she is going to be fine." Her words touched my heart and I knew they were true. I was finally able to feel peace.

Tiffani was released at 2:00 A.M. with a simple and final diagnosis of bad bruising. It felt good to wake up the next morning to a somewhat normal routine. I walked downstairs to let the dogs out, and for the first time I noticed Tiffani's doll lying in the dirt where Tiffani had fallen. I picked it up and went inside. Later that afternoon while I was talking to Tiffani about the accident, I asked her how she had fallen. She told me that she had made her baby doll fly like Chauncey and Tetet, and that the doll had fallen over the balcony. I looked at her seriously and, for the first time, tried to explain to her that Chauncey and Tetet were not real but were imaginary friends.

Tiffani was emphatic. She said, "No, Mommy, they are real and they play with me every day. They are my friends." I asked her what they looked like, and she replied, "They look like me but Chauncey has pink hair and Tetet has white hair and they have no feet, they just fly."

At this point, I was quite intrigued with what she was telling me. When I asked her why or how she had fallen off the balcony, she said that she was trying to get her baby doll. I asked her if she was scared while she was falling, and she said, "No, Mommy, Chauncey and Tetet helped to catch me after I fell off so I wouldn't get hurt."

A few days later, my mother had a similar discussion with Tiffani, and she repeated exactly the same account Tiffani had told me about her friends helping her. A few days later, Tiffani told me that Tetet had gone back to the mountains, but Chauncey stayed around for a couple more weeks and then returned to the mountains.

Tiffani is now five and very rarely talks about the incident. Chauncey and Tetet haven't been around for a long time, but I now believe they were with us for a time for a specific purpose. Tiffani came through the accident with one bruise the size of a dime on her left leg and a bad stomachache. I'm quite sure that if it hadn't been for her two loving guardian angels, her injuries would have been much more serious, and perhaps she wouldn't be with us today.

I hope the day will come when I can thank Chauncey and Tetet face to face for preserving the life of my precious daughter, and for giving me the privilege of being her mother a while longer.

A HELPING HAND

JOAN WESTER ANDERSON

Two-and-a-half-year-old Joey was an active child. From morning to night, he ran, climbed and jumped. Life was a glorious adventure—so much to see and do and explore!

Of course, it's difficult to keep such energetic children safe. Joey would act first and think later. But his mother Susie had rules, and most of the time her little son did his best to obey them.

One Saturday morning Susie was running errands in the car; Joey was strapped in his car seat behind her. As she drove down a particularly busy street Susie noticed a garage-sale sign.

"Oh, good!" She loved garage sales, so she pulled over and parked the car directly across the street from the sign. Carefully, she opened the driver's side door into traffic, got out, closed the door, and came around to the sidewalk.

Leaning inside, Susie lifted Joey out of his car seat and stood him on the sidewalk next to her. "Stay right here, honey," she reminded him.

Joey knew the rule about standing next to Mommy so he wouldn't get hurt or lost while she locked the car door. But there were so many exciting things to look at, and before Susie realized it, Joey had darted around her, between the parked cars, and out into the street.

He was almost to the center of the street when Susie looked up. "Joey!" she screamed. A truck was bearing down on him, coming far too fast to stop in time. A woman across the street at the garage sale saw what was happening and screamed, too. Susie started to run.

But as she dashed into the street she suddenly realized that Joey wasn't there any longer! Instead, he was standing against her car, facing the traffic, his arms outstretched along the car's side. As if he had been *placed* there. As if someone was shielding him.

How had this happened? She was too grateful to wonder. "Oh, Joey!" She gathered the little boy into her arms as she wept with relief. "Don't you ever do that again!"

It took a moment before Susie felt composed enough to walk across the street, and when she did, she clutched Joey's hand very tightly. As she approached the garage sale the woman came toward her. "When I saw that truck coming, I screamed," she began.

"I did, too." Susie nodded.

"He's such a lucky little guy," the woman went on. "Imagine what would have happened if that man hadn't pushed him out of the way."

Susie stopped, perplexed. "Man? What man?"

"He was older, and very tall," the woman explained. "I assumed he was with you, because he grabbed your child from the middle of the street, swung him over to the side of your car and stood in front of him."

"But what happened to the man?" Susie asked. "Where did he go?"

The woman looked around, her face puzzled. "Why, I don't know. He was there, and then he wasn't."

Susie was getting a funny feeling in her stomach. She knew very well she and Joey had been alone all day. Nor had she seen any man nearby. And yet, how had Joey ended up safely sheltered against the car?

"Each night I remind Joey to thank his guardian angel for keeping him safe," Susie now says. She does the same thing when she prays, too.

THE BLACK HOLE

JERRY B. JENKINS

As a child, one of the highlights of my week was playing tag in the parking lot after church on Sunday nights. We kids would burst from the tiny sanctuary of the Oakwood Baptist Church in Kalamazoo, Michigan, and race among the cars in the parking lot.

It wasn't that I didn't take church seriously. Church was a matter of course for us. After all, Sunday was the Lord's day. After breakfast we put on our best clothes and walked the three tree-lined blocks to Sunday school and morning worship. Sunday afternoon we played or read books. This day more than others I might ask Mom or Dad spiritual questions. Deep questions. Like *Can I really know I'm going to heaven?* Or *Do I really have a guardian angel?* My mother assured me that an angel was near me always. *What does the angel look like?* I'd ask. *Is it he or she? Big or little? Old or young?* Mother was like the others in the Oakwood Baptist Church milieu; angels were talked about but never seen.

Sunday evening we all walked along the sidewalk again, back to the white-frame, picture-postcard church for a less formal service. At night we were allowed to wear sneakers, unless I was singing a solo, which I did on occasion. My premiere was a bold performance of a favorite children's song, "I Met Jesus at the Crossroads."

During the evening sermon I wrote notes to my brothers. We all chewed on the Life Savers Mother kept in her purse. And we waited for the last verse of the last hymn so we could run to the dark parking lot filled with Chevys and Fords for our wild game of tag.

In 1960, when I was ten, I was the youngest and smallest of the Sunday night regular tag players—boys and girls, ages ten to fourteen. My size gave me one advantage: I had a knack for being best able to slip through the crowd and out the door. Once I heard that final amen, I would "walk—don't run" down the back steps, through the foyer, the first to step foot onto the sidewalk. And once I was outside, I ran. The game had begun.

One particular fall night, our family filled a row near the back. So far so good. And I had maneuvered myself into a seat at the end of the pew, closest to the door. At the crack of dismissal, I leapt out into the aisle, down the stairs and out into a pitch dark night.

Yes! I made it. No one was even close behind me. By habit I took a hard left, along a sidewalk close to the building, and sprinted with all my might toward the parking lot.

Just past the edge of the building, where the sidewalk ended—wham! An arm as firm as oak caught me in the stomach. My hands and feet flew out ahead of me, but the arm held me upright until I could stand again. Dazed, with my breath slowly coming back, I looked down at a sight I could hardly believe: I was standing, teetering, at the edge of a huge, deep crater.

I staggered back. Then I remembered. The parking lot had been excavated that week. I myself had watched the bulldozer dig the foundation for a new sanctuary. I'd played sidewalk supervisor as Dad and others had slid a truckload of cinder blocks down a wooden ramp and made piles of them in that hole. I'd helped deliver soft drinks Mom had sent over.

With rubbery legs I slunk back toward the church door. By now my friends were out and running, away from the construction site, off to the right and around toward the big backyard. And now I saw the usually empty street lined with the cars that would have been in the parking lot. I was too shaken to join in the play. For a long time I just stood near the front door, thinking about what might have happened. I would have fallen in, would have hit those cinder blocks, been knocked out cold. The night was so dark, no one would have found me until morning. By then it would have been too late. Now my wild imagination took over. I pictured the headlines: *Jenkins Boy Found Dead.*

But the arm that had saved my life—whose arm was it? Big Walt Burke, my Sunday school teacher? With his bulk, he could have stopped me. And he did sometimes hang around outside and warn us kids, including his daughters, to be careful. No. He was just coming out now.

Old Mr. Kemple, the church patriarch who looked the part of a Southern gentleman? But he was too small and frail to have held me back. I would have run him down. And he was still inside.

The truth was I'd been saved by something I couldn't see. By someone I couldn't see. I couldn't explain the mystery and it scared me.

When we got home my older brothers asked what was wrong with me. *Nothing. Leave me alone. Why don't you mind your own business?* If I told them, they would laugh, if not at my reckless stupidity then at my vivid imagination.

I did tell my mother, at least part of the story. "After church I almost fell in the hole," I said. But I couldn't tell her about being caught up short by an invisible arm—that was too spooky to admit. Only as the years went by did I begin to connect that arm at my waist with the guardian angel I had always wondered about. My mother's assurances of divine protection had proven more firm than she had ever imagined.

Today I no longer sing church solos. I no longer leap down the church steps, trying to be the first one out. We don't live within walking distance of our church. I now have sons of my own, and churchgoing has not changed a lot from those years in the sixties at Oakwood Baptist. Today, at Village Church in Gurnee, Illinois, with a voice very much like my dad's, I admonish my sons to walk—don't run—inside God's house. If the service runs long, my wife hands breath mints down our row. When they hear the last amen, my boys make a beeline for the back door.

And late at night, I see my boyhood self in my sons, afraid, sometimes, of the dark. When the bogeyman lurks in the bedroom closet or outside the window, I assure them the closet is safe, the windows are secured. As a parent I'll do my best to protect them. As for the things a parent can't see or control, we trust those things to God. Then I tell them my story about the night I almost fell into the black hole. About the arm that held me back from disaster.

I quote from a psalm from the King James Bible I heard as a child: "For he shall give his angels charge over thee, to keep in all thy ways. They shall bear thee up in their hands, lest thou dash thy foot against a stone" (Psalm 91:11-12, KJV).

These things, my child, never change.

Chapter 5
God Sends His Angels to Rescue Us

Let us help each other by our prayers,
so that God and Christ and the whole choir of angels,
may come to our aid in our time of suffering,
when we shall need their assistance the most.

—Nemesian of Numidia

Life is extremely fragile. Most of us move blithely through our lives, blessedly ignorant of the dangers that threaten us daily. But each of us has also experienced that split-second of terror when our sense of safety and well-being is shattered by peril: the near-miss bicycle accident, finding your child with an open prescription bottle, a grease fire that flares up without warning.

Many people face personal peril on a daily basis; they are victims of war or terrorism or abuse or live in neighborhoods controlled by gangs. Safety is a elusive luxury and an illusion that can be quickly shattered.

Remember Daniel in the lion's den?

Daniel was tossed into the den of lions when he violated King Darius's law prohibiting prayer to anyone but the king himself. A stone was placed over the top of the den and the king placed his seal on the stone so no one would interfere to help

Daniel. After a sleepless night, Darius hurried back to the lion's den, and called out, "Daniel, servant of the living God, has your God, whom you serve continually, been able to rescue you from the lions?" Imagine the king's shock to hear Daniel's call, "O king, live forever! My God sent his angel, and he shut the mouths of the lions."

What a story! The God who sent an angel to rescue Daniel has promised to rescue us when we face danger. The stories that follow are celebrations of God's faithfulness to His children in their times of peril.

> If you make the Most High your dwelling—
> even the LORD, who is my refuge—
> then no harm will befall you,
> no disaster will come near your tent.
> For he will command his angels concerning you
> to guard you in all your ways;
> they will lift you up in their hands,
> so that you will not strike your foot against a stone.
>
> —Psalm 91:9-12

PINNED BY A BULL

LORRAINE ZURLIENE

Even though I knew what time it was, I rolled over and glared at the clock: 5:45 A.M., milking time. I sighed. It was getting harder each day to get out of bed. In a month I would turn fifty. Birthdays usually don't bother me, but lately I was in a rut. Cornel and I had had our first six children in six years. Eight years later Tricia and Cindi, now teenagers, had come along. Much as I love my family, I sometimes wondered if I would ever finish keeping house, milking cows and raising kids. Were these my only objectives in life?

Dragging myself from bed, I gathered my barn clothes from a peg by the stairs. In the mild, early November weather all I needed was a sweatshirt, light cotton pants, socks and white tennis shoes. Still groggy, I paused on the side porch and looked to the east across a harvested soybean field where the lightening sky silhouetted dark, distant trees. Surrounding the house lay two hundred and fifty acres that had been farmed by Cornel's family for two generations. I hurried across the wide gravel drive separating the house and barn, revived by a chilly west wind.

In the barn Cornel had already brought the automatic milkers from the milk house and started attaching them to the overhead pipes and air hoses.

"You go on to work," I said. Cornel needed to leave for his trucking job by 6:15.

"I will, as soon as the girls get here. I've told you before. You must have someone with you in the barn, Lorraine." Cornel repeated his familiar warning: "Livestock is unpredictable."

"I've got my stick." I held up a length of heavy broomstick. "If a cow gives me any trouble, a whack on the nose will take care of it."

Cornel shook his head and scooped a mixture of grain and molasses into the feed trough while I guided each black and white Holstein's head into a stanchion, adjusted the yoke and pulled the lever latching her into place. I moved down the line, touching each cow on the hip to let her know I was there before I attached the milker. Soon there was a rhythmic hiss-swoosh of the vacuum lines overhead and milk flowed through a glass tube into an adjoining room. There a tank held the milk at a constant thirty-eight degrees.

Just in time, Tricia and Cindi hurried into the barn to take over for Cornel. Before leaving, he reminded me, "Keep the girls here until you finish."

"I don't like making the girls late for school," I mumbled.

"Then wait for Kirk to get here." Our son Kirk worked nights and came home about midmorning. That was too late; I could have the milking done before then.

After Cornel had been gone a few minutes, I told Tricia and Cindi they could go get ready for school. At 7:20 they yelled, "Bye, Mom," and got on their school bus.

I liked being alone with the cows. They didn't talk back. They seemed to enjoy it when I sang to them, as long as I didn't stay in the high soprano range, like the time I practiced the "Hallelujah Chorus." That caused them to jump or kick. Today, with no one present for miles around, I launched into "How Great Thou Art."

Then I noticed two unmilked cows huddled with a young bull in the center of the seventy-by-two hundred-foot barnyard. Motioning and calling to the cows brought no results, so I walked toward them. "C'mon, now. Get in the barn. Get in there," I coaxed. They stuck close by the bull. Then the bull took a threatening step my way.

A feeling of uneasiness swept over me; the nearest fence was thirty-five feet away. The bull weighed at least fifteen hundred pounds and could outrun anyone. I decided to take no chances. This bull was young and had given us no real problems before. I could scare him away. I lifted my broomstick club and brought it down hard on his nose, expecting him to back off. Instead he charged. His head slammed into my chest. My torso recoiled, my back arched and I was off my feet and on my backside. I tried to get up and scramble away, but he pursued, pounding my legs with his head.

"Help! Help!" I screamed. "Somebody help me!"

But even if a car drove by on our isolated blacktop road, the silos were blocking me from view. I knew no one would hear or see me.

Methodically the bull hammered my legs from ankles to hip, ramming his massive head again and again. One flimsy tennis shoe flew off.

The bull moved forward so he stood directly over me, his eyes so dark they were almost blue-black. Rolling his eyes, he pitched his head and brought it down on me, his breath hot on my legs. Writhing in the loose dirt I tried to escape, but my ankle was pinned beneath his huge split hoof.

Covering my head with my arm, I closed my eyes and turned on my side. The aroma of loamy, dry dirt rose and mixed with the sharp smell of manure. Any moment I expected my ribs to be snapped, my chest crushed.

This is the end. I'm going to die.

I gave up and quit screaming.

Instantly, warmth and comfort enveloped me. Even though my eyes were closed, I sensed a pink cloud of loving protection. With no fear, no cares, I relaxed and felt at peace. Content in my pink cloud, I waited for the bull's killing blows. And waited. Nothing happened.

Finally, I opened my eyes and was shocked to see that the bull had retreated about twelve feet. He stood there, body rigid, eyes fixed in my direction.

When he didn't move, I sat up. He started to make a run but immediately halted, focused on something in the space between us. I could feel my pink cloud. Was the bull also aware of it?

I struggled to my feet. The bull remained frozen in place. With my trampled ankle sending pain shooting up my leg, I hobbled toward the fence. The bull stood there as if paralyzed, staring at me.

Desperately I glanced toward the barbed-wire fence, still thirty feet away, but mainly I kept my eye on the mesmerized bull. Nearing the fence, trying to run, I stumbled, lurched and limped toward it. At last, crawling, I slid under the barbed wire and scurried behind a nearby tree for protection.

As soon as I reached safety, the bull came to life. Lowering his head, he snorted and pawed the ground. Kicking up dirt, he galloped straight for the fence. The fence was strong and I was beyond his reach. With a final, angry snort, his ears twitching and his tail flicking, the bull trotted away.

I was injured and knew I couldn't do the milking. *What about the cows?* I wondered. *What would they do when I didn't return?*

As I shuffled toward the driveway, Kirk pulled in. Relieved to see him home early, I said, "That young bull got me down and beat me up. I'm going to the house. Can you finish the milking?"

He looked concerned and started firing questions, but I said sternly, "I'm okay. You go on and milk those cows."

I sat on the sofa and checked my legs. They were already beginning to swell, and I felt lumps rising from the deep bruises. Out the windows, across the field to the east, I saw the same dark trees I had seen earlier. Now they stood in full sunshine. I inhaled deeply—no broken ribs. All at once it struck me: *I'm alive!* I could hardly believe it. A person alone attacked by a bull doesn't stand a chance. How had I escaped? Something had stopped the bull from mauling me; something had saved me. And that something had surrounded me and felt like a pink cloud.

Several times for family and friends I repeated the story of what had happened. I told about the bull, but how can you explain that an angel in the form of a pink cloud saved your life?

I had spent all my days farming, cooking, cleaning and caring for children until I thought there was nothing more to look forward to. And then an angel came along to prove me wrong. *If my life was saved,* I thought, *I must have a lot of purpose left, a lot to get out of bed for in the mornings.*

In five weeks the pain and swelling subsided enough for me to return to the barnyard. There in the dirt I found my tennis shoe. Like me, it looked pretty beat up. I retrieved it, and I took it inside to clean. We had work to do, and I had life to look forward to.

SKY-HIGH ADVENTURE

ANNA-MARIE WEAD

Since New Year's I'd dreamed of nothing else. For the second January in a row our family had come to Telluride, Colorado, for a ski vacation, and I couldn't wait to get back on the slopes. I'd spent much of our 1984 trip taking lessons, but soon enough I'd mastered turning, stopping and shifting my weight from leg to leg. People say, the younger you are, the easier it is. I was four years old, and totally fearless shooting down the hill. Skiing was awesome!

Now a year later I was wearing my red skis and waiting with my mother for the chair lift. Getting on and off scared me, so I stuck by Mom. "We'll do it together," she said.

We moved along double file with the other skiers, everybody bundled up against the cold in bright-colored outfits. I was on Mom's right so I'd be closest to the lift attendant. He'd help me when our chair arrived.

I handed my pole to Mom and went over in my mind all I was supposed to do: Look across my shoulder at the chair as the attendant boosted me up into the seat, grab the chair arm, and then sit back so Mom could clamp the bar shut. Whew! Once you're in the seat, the ride is great. I loved looking down; my skis dangling in the air, watching people crisscross the slopes below.

As Mom and I neared the head of the line, I wriggled around her legs, peering up at the mountain. I couldn't stand still, thinking of the fun I was going to have. The line moved fast, and the chairs whipped by. Our turn came, and I suddenly found myself on Mom's left side instead of her right—she would be standing between me and the attendant! "Mom!"

She twisted around as she secured the poles and pulled herself into the seat. "Anna-Marie!" she screamed, a look of horror on her face. I reached for her, but the rising chair hit me in the back. Mom leaned down, grabbing me by the arms, yanking me out from under the chair. "Stop the lift!" she shouted, holding on to me for dear life.

The lift did not stop. I hung in my mother's grip like a rag doll as the cables spun, and the chairs rose higher. I felt so heavy, my skis dragging me down. I glanced up at Mom, who was doubled over in the chair, fighting desperately to keep her hold on me.

"Don't move, honey," she said. "I've got you. I won't let you go. I promise."

I looked down at the skiers as they swooshed to a halt and pointed at me. "Stop the lift!" they yelled. The wind whistled as the chair rose into the air. We passed one of the steel columns supporting the cables. Then we went by another. Then a third, higher than the one before. The ground fell farther and farther away.

"Don't be afraid," Mom said. "God is with us." I believed her. My mom was right about everything. I saw that she was praying, so I prayed too. Her hands pressed into me. As long as I kept looking at my mom, I felt safe.

Finally, the chair lift jerked to a stop. Mom struggled to keep her balance, pulling back, clasping me tighter. There were loud cries from below. People called out. *What's happening?* I wondered. Then a shout: "Someone's coming!" I looked up. A man was hanging from the icy cables with his bare hands. He was swinging toward us, hand over hand, just like an acrobat I'd seen at the circus. When he was directly above us, he let go of the cables and, without even rocking the chair, he landed in front of Mom, his small feet perched on the edge of the seat.

"What do we have here?" he asked, grinning at me. He told me to hold on and gripped the shoulders of my ski suit. Mom released me and leaned back in the chair. With one quick motion, the man raised me up in his strong arms. He sat me in the seat, but stood between Mom and me. We heard cheers from the crowd below, and Mom reached around to hug my shoulder. Then the lift began to move again.

"Are you okay?" Mom asked, her eyes full of tears. I nodded, and looked into the man's ruddy face. Mom thanked him over and over. "Where did you come from?" she asked. "From the restaurant," he answered. "I'm the cook." It felt as if we'd been friends for a long time, so I grabbed his hand. It was warm! He didn't seem to be cold at all, though he wore only jeans and a shirt—no coat, hat or gloves. I couldn't figure out how he had seen us all the way from the kitchen.

In minutes we were at the top of the mountain, and the skiers ahead of us jumped out of their chairs. "Here we go!" Mom said as she and I slid onto the snow. The man wasn't wearing skis so he stayed on the lift. People gathered around Mom and me, but we turned to catch sight of the descending chairs. We saw the man wave as the cables spun his chair away from us.

Mom and I dug in our poles, and we glided down the slope under the ski lift, glancing up, searching for our new friend. But all the chairs headed downward were empty. When we reached the bottom we went to the restaurant, hoping to see the cook again. No one—not the cook or anyone else employed at the resort—fit the man's description or knew who he was.

I still remember everything about that day, especially when I go skiing with my mom. "Don't be afraid," she'd said. "God is with us." As always, she was right.

SAFELY HOME

JOAN WESTER ANDERSON

I t was just past midnight on December 24, 1983. The Midwest was shivering through a record-breaking cold spell, complete with gale-force winds and frozen water pipes. And although our suburban Chicago household was filled with the snug sounds of a family at rest, I couldn't be a part of them, not until our twenty-one-year-old son pulled into the driveway. At the moment, Tim and his two room-mates were driving home for Christmas, their first trip back since they had moved East last May. "Don't worry, Mom," Tim had reassured me over the phone last night. "We're going to leave before dawn tomorrow and drive straight through. We'll be fine!"

Kids. They do insane things. Under normal circumstances, I figured, a Connecticut-to-Illinois trek ought to take about eighteen hours. But the weather had turned so dangerously cold that radio reports warned against venturing outdoors, even for a few moments. And then we had heard nothing from the travelers. Distressed, I pictured them on a desolate road. What if they ran into car problems or lost their way? And if they *had* been delayed, why hadn't Tim phoned? Restlessly I paced and prayed in the familiar shorthand all mothers know: *God, send someone to help them.*

By now, as I later learned, the trio had stopped briefly in Fort Wayne, Indiana, to deposit Don at his family home. Common sense suggested that Tim and Jim stay the rest of the night and resume their trek in the morning. But when does common sense prevail with invincible young adults? There were only four driving hours left to reach home. And although it was the coldest night in Midwest history and the highways were snowy and deserted, the two had started out again.

They had been traveling for only a few miles on a rural access road to the Indiana tollway when they noticed that the car's engine seemed sluggish, lurching erratically and dying to ten or fifteen miles per hour. Tim glanced uneasily at Jim. "Do not—" the radio announcer intoned, "—repeat—do not venture outside tonight, friends. There's a record wind-chill of eighty below zero, which means that exposed skin will freeze in less than a minute." The car surged suddenly, then coughed and slowed again.

"Tim," Jim spoke into the darkness, "we're not going to stall here, are we?"

"We can't," Tim answered grimly as he pumped the accelerator. "We'll die for sure."

But instead of picking up speed, the engine sputtered, chugging and slowing again. About a mile later, at the top of a small incline, the car crawled to a frozen stop.

Horrified, Tim and Jim looked at each other in the darkened interior. They could see across the fields in every direction, but, incredibly, theirs was the only vehicle in view. For the first time, they faced the fact that they were in enormous danger. There was no traffic, no refuge ahead, not even a farmhouse light blinking in the distance. It was as if they had landed on an alien, snow-covered planet.

And the appalling, unbelievable cold! Never in Tim's life had he experienced anything so intense. They couldn't run for help; he knew that for sure. He and Jim were young and strong, but even if shelter were only a short distance away, they couldn't survive. The temperature would kill them in a matter of minutes.

"Someone will come along soon," Jim muttered, looking in every direction. "They are bound to."

"I don't think so," Tim said. "You heard the radio. Everyone in the world is inside tonight—except us."

"Then what are we going to do?"

"I don't know." Tim tried starting the engine again, but the ignition key clicked hopelessly in the silence. Bone-chilling cold penetrated the car's interior, and his feet were already growing numb. *Well, God,* he prayed, echoing my own distant plea, *You're the only one who can help us now.*

It seemed impossible to stay awake much longer. Then, as if they had already slipped into a dream, they saw headlights flashing at the car's rear. But that was impossible. For they had seen no twin pinpricks of light in the distance, no hopeful approach. Where had the vehicle come from? Had they already died?

But no. For, miraculously, someone was knocking on the driver's side window. "Need to be pulled?" In disbelief they heard the muffled shout. But it was true. Their rescuer was driving a tow truck.

"Yes! Oh, yes, thanks!" Quickly, the two conferred as the driver, saying nothing more, drove around to the front of the car and attached chains. If there were no garages open at this hour, they would ask him to take them back to Don's house, where they could spend the rest of the night.

Swathed almost completely in a furry parka, hood and a scarf up to his eyes, the driver nodded at their request but said nothing more. He was calm, they noted as he climbed into his truck, seemingly unconcerned about the life-threatening circumstances in which he had found them. *Strange that he's not curious about us*, Tim mused, *and isn't even explaining where he came from or how he managed to approach without our seeing him.* And had there been any lettering on the side of the truck? Tim hadn't noticed any. *He's going to give us a big bill, on a night like this. I'll have to borrow some money from Don or his dad.* But Tim was exhausted from the ordeal, and gradually, as he leaned against the seat, his thoughts slipped away.

They passed two locked service stations, stopped to alert Don from a pay phone, and were soon being towed back through the familiar Fort Wayne neighborhood. With Christmas lights long since extinguished and families asleep, Don's still seemed the most welcoming street they had ever been on. The driver maneuvered carefully around the cul-de-sac and pulled up in front of Don's house. Numb with cold, Tim and Jim raced to the side door where Don was waiting, then tumbled into the blessedly warm kitchen, safe at last.

"The tow truck driver, Don—I have to pay him. I need to borrow—"

"Wait a minute." Don frowned, looking past his friends through the window. "I don't see any tow truck out there."

Tim and Jim turned around. There, parked alone at the curb, was Tim's car. There had been no sound in the crystal-clear night of its release from the chains, no door slam, no chug of an engine pulling away. There had been no bill for Tim to pay, no receipt to sign, no farewell or "thank you" or "Merry Christmas." Stunned, Tim raced back down the driveway to the curb, but there were no taillights disappearing in the distance, no engine noise echoing through the silent streets, nothing at all to mark the tow truck's presence.

Then Tim saw the tire tracks traced in the windblown snowdrifts. But there was only one set of marks ringing the cul-de-sac curve. And they belonged to Tim's car. . . .

RESCUE ON ROSARITO BEACH

MARK ABRAM

We have beautiful lakes and good ol' swimming holes in Wisconsin, but there's nothing to equal an ocean. Last summer I accompanied twenty teenagers on a mission trip to Tijuana, Mexico. Everyone looked forward to achieving our goal of building modest houses for two homeless Mexican families, but we also anticipated one of the perks of the trip: an afternoon by the Pacific Ocean.

I'm a pastor of one of three churches in the Appleton, Wisconsin area that participate in the annual event, and this year I was asked to go along. "Please come with us, Dad!" begged my sixteen-year-old daughter Jilly. Looking into her eager face, I realized how quickly my little girl was growing into a young woman.

Will she always need her dad as she does now? I wondered. This trip was a chance for us to share an experience we'd never forget. "Count on me," I said.

The kids were psyched as we flew into San Diego, California, that Friday last July. It was late in the evening when we finally traveled through the Tijuana border gate, and then on to the place where we'd be staying. Saturday we got to know our Mexican co-workers, and precut some lumber for the houses we'd build during the coming week. Jilly threw herself into the job, and I watched how her enthusiasm sparked everyone she worked with. This take-charge person is my daughter, I thought with pride.

After church on Sunday, we headed for a local restaurant and then to the beach. "*Rosarito es muy bueno,*" Jilly and I had been told by our new Mexican friends. "Rosarito Beach is very good." So that was our destination, a suburb about fifteen miles down the coast from our compound in Tijuana. Rosarito is a large resort area favored by Californians, but we'd been directed to a quiet area of the beach locals liked. Sure enough, most of the beachgoers were Mexicans speaking exuberant Spanish.

Our bunch was just as excited in teenage English seeing the ocean for the first time. "Wow!" "Awesome!" "Cool!" The kids raced down the beach. Adults who'd been on the trip in previous summers had warned us that the breezes were typically chilly and the ocean cold. Rarely did anyone venture into the water. But on this day several of the boys, Jilly and two other girls called upon their native pride. With a resoluteness formed by a lifetime of freezing Wisconsin winters, they were ready to challenge the sea. "Here we go, Dad!" shouted Jilly, and she and her friends splashed in. Powerful four-foot waves surged toward the beach. I followed the kids in.

I grew up in Florida, and I spent my own teenage days surfing the waves at Cocoa Beach. As a result, I have a healthy respect for the ocean. "Don't go any farther out, you guys," I told Jilly and the kids. East Coast or West, Atlantic or Pacific, oceans are all the same. There's a hidden current along the beach, the undertow. It pulls in the opposite direction, headed out to sea as the waves crash on shore, and you don't want to get caught in it.

Our group had thinned out to Jilly and me and five boys—Travis, Kyle, Kurt, Chris and Josh. We were body-surfing in about four feet of water by a sandbar. There didn't seem to be any undertow, but I'd felt a current pulling us northward. After a half hour or so, I noticed the seven of us were easily two hundred yards beyond where we'd entered the water. Jilly was having the time of her life, and I hated to put an end to the fun.

Then Travis yelled, "Help!"

He was frantically treading water, trying to stay afloat. Before I could do anything I lost my footing and started to sink. I couldn't find the sandbar.

"Dad!" Jilly screamed. I whipped around. My daughter was being pulled below the surface.

"Undertow!" I shouted. Kyle and Kurt, about twenty yards south of us, started paddling for shore with all their might. Chris and Josh swam toward Travis. What if the three of them were swept out to sea? We all needed help, desperately. Dear God, I prayed, where are You?

I grabbed Jilly into my arms. It was all I could do to lift her head above water as the swells tried to drag us down. I knew the undertow could be beaten by first swimming parallel to the shore and then toward it, but I couldn't do that and also tow my daughter to safety.

Were there lifeguards nearby? I didn't remember seeing them. Would anyone risk his life to save us? There were only a few people on the beach. Did any of them realize we were in trouble? Could they hear our cries for help over the roar of the waves? The current was too strong for me to fight much longer. I hugged my daughter as close as I could and tread water. Her face was white with fear. "I'm here, Jilly," I said. What more could I do? Jilly knew she had my love, but it wasn't enough. I had my faith, but was that enough? "God is here," I whispered to my daughter, wanting to believe with all my heart that it was true.

A large swell rose in front of us, and at its crest swam a Mexican fellow in a red bathing suit. He came toward us, pulling a small red float. Behind him, in single file, were two more young men, pulling the same red floats and wearing identical red bathing suits. Lifeguards!

The first swimmer reached us, calling out, "*¡Señor! ¡Señorita!*" as the other two swam toward the boys. We grabbed the float and kicked our feet, trying to help propel ourselves. "No!" our lifeguard called as he towed us toward shore. He wanted us to relax and let him bring us in. But I couldn't help it. I kicked my feet with every last bit of strength I had.

We staggered onto the beach and I fell to my knees. A magnificent sight awaited me. All five boys had safely reached shore. My daughter was next to me, smiling that sweet smile I loved so much. I grabbed the hands of our savior. "*¡Gracias!*" I said, happily using the little Spanish I knew. "*¡Muchas gracias!*" Were words of thanks enough? I made the universal sign of doling out cash and said, "*Dinero.*" The young lifeguard shook his head, and waved to his red-suited companions. "It's all right," he said in perfect English. "It's my job."

So off we went, trudging back to the rest of our party down the beach. As Jilly and the boys relayed the events, I decided to return to the spot where we'd been rescued. I wanted to thank the lifeguards again. For the next half hour I searched. But I found nothing, not even those red floats in an official-looking pile. During the week as we completed our house-building project, I asked our Mexican friends about Rosarito Beach. They said they'd never seen lifeguards there. Back in Wisconsin, a church member who has made several trips to Tijuana told me the same thing, and I finally embraced the reality of our rescue. Human families have an everlasting bond, but we are all children of God. Proof of His love can sweep in like a wave from the ocean.

AS TALL AS TREES

MARILYNN CARLSON WEBBER AND WILLIAM D. WEBBER

A couple of years ago, Tina Lee's husband David was clearing some land to enlarge their produce garden near their home in rural Georgia. The Lees enjoy gardening, and their crops of peas, butterbeans, tomatoes and potatoes (among other things) fed them year 'round. As David drove the tractor, Tina went inside to answer the telephone, which was by a window from which she could watch both her husband and their two-year-old son Joshua, who was playing near the house.

As she picked up the phone, she was horrified to look outside and see David on the ground—and the tractor on top of him.

"Joshua, stay right there!" she yelled to her son as she raced past him to try to save her husband.

Tina arrived to find the tractor pinning David by the rubber sole of his work boot. The ignition key was turned halfway to off, which had stalled the large tractor. Tina immediately climbed up and turned off the motor, then she helped David out from under the tractor, and together they were able to right it. The worst injury he suffered was a twisted ankle.

As they discussed the accident, David shook his head and said he didn't understand what had happened: He remembered the tractor's being right over him— then moving away from him as if someone had shoved it aside. He also had no idea why the engine had stalled when it did. He had expected to lose his leg if not his life.

Just then little Joshua came running over to his parents.

"Did you see him, Daddy?" Joshua asked.

"Who?"

"The man," the little boy said, his eyes still wide. "He was as tall as the trees! He moved the tractor when it was falling on Daddy, then he turned the key."

Tina and David hadn't seen, but they both knew that "from the mouths of babes" had come the only explanation for what had happened. "I've always believed in angels and felt their comfort," says Tina, "but this solidified my belief that angels are always protecting us, too!"

UNLIKELY VISITORS

JAN SMITH

We were both born-and-bred Texans, but in 1964 my husband Howard and I were thinking of moving somewhere else. Howard was just out of the Marines, and in June we visited some of his old buddies in northern California while we looked for work there. You could say things were up in the air with us. When we finally headed back to Texas, nothing had been decided about our future, and I was feeling down.

Checking the road map as we crossed into Nevada, I had an idea. "How about some fun?" I asked. "We could see the Grand Canyon." We would have to turn north and go out of our way, but Howard's face brightened. "Let's go!" he said.

We'd always wanted to visit the Grand Canyon, often poring over pictures of it at home and dreaming of a trip. But pictures and dreams can't begin to prepare you for the real thing. I couldn't believe my eyes when we first entered the park. *God's creation in all its wonder*, I thought, as we stared across the boundless space from the canyon's rim.

The weather was warm and I was glad I'd worn only my favorite red shorts and a cool shirt. We opened the windows wide to catch the breeze as we drove along the park's southern edge. About every fifteen minutes I called, "Stop here!" and jumped out of the car to take a picture. My clothes and white tennis shoes were soon brown with dust, but I didn't care.

I was almost out of film by the time we reached the southeastern corner of the canyon. "One last picture!" I begged, spotting a beautiful lookout point below a thick hedge just off the road. Howard pulled over and I leaped from the car. I ran behind the hedge and down three steps toward a landing enclosed by an iron guardrail. As I stepped onto the landing with my right foot, the rubber sole of my shoe crunched on a thick layer of pea-sized gravel. Holding tight to the camera around my neck, I tried to regain my balance, but my foot flew out from under me. I fell on my back, my legs in the air, and began to slide across the gravel. The landing sloped at a forty-five degree angle, and I couldn't stop myself. I was heading feet first toward the canyon's waiting mouth.

Grab the guardrail! I reached for the lower iron bar of the rail—but missed. I was so skinny I went right under it. The camera swung wildly and smashed against the canyon wall, film unspooling into the wind, the cord pressing at my neck. I felt my head leave the edge of the landing. Scrub brush growing from the canyon wall tore at me as I slid downward. All I could see was sky above and the open canyon below.

I stretched my arms high over my head, reaching up—hoping, praying, trying to stop myself from sliding. I was grabbing at the air! If I could only find something to hold onto. . . .

A hand! Someone caught my wrist in a powerful grip, instantly stopping my slide down the wall. There was no struggle, no jerk of my body. My shoulders and back pressed against the rock.

"Are you okay, my dear?" asked a tall old man with white hair. He had soft eyes and a healthy glow to his face. He smiled a grandfatherly smile, and I knew I could trust him with my life. "Up we go," he said. And with one swift movement I was lifted out of the canyon and laid safely on the gravel landing. How could anyone so old be so strong?

Catching my breath, I looked more closely at my rescuer. The man was probably in his seventies. His clothes were old-fashioned and carefully pressed. I admired his stiff white shirt with a tall collar and wide tie. His polished black shoes were long and narrow, and laced up with neatly tied bows. Stooping beside him was an old lady, looking at me with twinkling dark eyes. She wore a long print dress, tight around her neck with a lace collar draped in a semicircle down to her ample bosom. There was a cameo at the center of her throat. Her hose were thick and black, her high-top shoes shiny with a wide heel. The man and woman were picture-perfect, not a speck of dust on either of them.

The woman enfolded me in her arms. She and her companion helped my to my feet, cooing over me, trying to soothe me. They straightened my clothes and took the broken camera from my neck. When I calmed down, they moved to either side of me and we walked up the steps and around the hedge. Howard was waiting patiently in the car. Only a few minutes had elapsed. He knew nothing of what had happened until he saw me.

I winced as he put me in the car. "You'll find help for her there," the man said, pointing up the road to the left. "It's a hospital," added the woman.

"Thank you!" Howard said, closing my door and hurrying behind the wheel. "Thank you," I called as strongly as I could. We turned to wave at the elderly couple as we drove away. They walked toward the landing, and disappeared behind the hedge.

"Where did they go?" Howard asked. "Where did they come from?" I countered. Two old people dressed in some kind of outdated Sunday best—unlikely clothes for canyon visitors. And the man couldn't have been standing on the ledge when he grabbed my wrist. I'd slid too far to be reached from there. Had he been climbing around the steep walls of the canyon? Impossible!

The hospital was just where the couple told us it would be. Doctors and attendants treated me, cleaning my wounds, meticulously picking gravel from all over my body. They found scrapes from scrub brush on my head, neck and shoulders. They all shook their heads in disbelief. This was proof to them that I had indeed fallen into the canyon.

Today I see the old couple as clearly in my mind as I did when they stood on either side of me, all those years ago. Back then Howard and I decided the best thing to do was to stay put for the time being. And in the end Texas has always been home. But that doesn't mean I haven't seen other changes in my life. Always, though, when insecurities leave me up in the air, I remember God's steadying grip.

Chapter 6
God Sends His Angels to Protect Us

When the servant of the man of God got up and went out early the next morning, an army with horses and chariots had surrounded the city. "Oh, my lord, what shall we do?" the servant asked.

"Don't be afraid," the prophet answered. "Those who are with us are more than those who are with them."

And Elisha prayed, "O LORD, open his eyes so he may see." Then the LORD opened the servant's eyes, and he looked and saw the hills full of horses and chariots of fire all around Elisha (2 Kings 6:15-17).

✳

It's so very easy to think of angels as "nice" angels. You know the kind: angels who hover over the earth while singing and plucking celestial instruments. Angels whose eyes are closed in rapture or who gently soothe a child to sleep. These tame angels are the sort we feel we can talk to, relate to—these angels are *safe*.

In truth, most of the angelic encounters reported in Scripture open with the admonishment, "Don't be afraid!" The most natural response to meeting an angel is very likely Zachariah's: "He was startled and gripped with fear." And why not? Angels are fearsome creatures who live in the presence of God and serve as agents of the Creator Himself.

When we're in danger we naturally cry out to God for protection. Angels are dispatched to do battle for us, very often in ways we cannot imagine—or even see! When Elisha frustrated the attempts of the king of Aram to crush the armies of Israel, the king ordered his troops to capture Elisha, who was living in the city of Dothan. The troops amassed outside the city, awaiting orders. When Elisha's fearful servant pointed out their situation, Elisha prayed that the servant would see the true situation: covering the hills surrounding the city were horses and chariots of fire, the hosts of God sent to defend the man of God.

What follows here are stories of angelic warriors who are dispatched by a loving Father Who protects His own, just as a parent safeguards a child.

> I sought the LORD, and he answered me;
> he delivered me from all my fears. . .
> The angel of the LORD encamps around those who fear him,
> and he delivers them.
> Taste and see that the LORD is good;
> blessed is the man who takes refuge in him.
>
> —Psalm 34:4, 6, 8

MIGHTY WARRIORS DRESSED FOR BATTLE

WILLIAM D. WEBBER AND MARILYNN CARLSON WEBBER

There have been times when lives were changed by an encounter with warrior angels. One well-documented case occurred in the life of John Patton.

John Patton and his wife were pioneer missionaries to the New Hebrides Islands. Faithfully they tried to live out the Christian gospel and model a Christian lifestyle. They were met with hostility. They returned insults with kindness, hatred with love.

It soon became apparent that even their lives were in danger. There were threats that their home would be burned and the missionary couple murdered, but the Pattons felt called by God. Praying for divine protection, they continued to minister in a spirit of love.

Then one night they heard noises outside their small missionary compound. Looking out, they saw they were completely surrounded by the chief and his men with torches and spears. They were being true to their word. They had come to burn their home and kill the missionaries. The Pattons had no weapons. There were no earthly means of protection, but they could pray, and pray they did! Throughout the terror-filled night they prayed for God to send His angels to protect them. They prayed that this warlike tribe would someday find peace with God.

When the morning came, the tribe silently left. The Pattons were elated but very surprised. There seemed to be no reason for the war party to leave.

Others of fainter heart would have sailed away from the island looking for more hospitable mission territory, but the Pattons felt called by God to stay. Fearlessly yet gently and lovingly, they continued to witness but without any noticeable results.

A full year later, the chief became a Christian. Finally John Patton was able to ask the question that had puzzled him for so long: "Chief, remember that night you came and surrounded our house? Your men all had spears and torches. What had you planned to do?"

The chief replied, "We came to kill you and burn everything you have."

"What kept you from doing it?" the missionary asked.

"We were afraid of all those men who were guarding your house," the chief replied.

"But there were no men," Patton replied. "We were alone, my wife and I."

"No, no," the chief insisted. "There were many men around your house. Big men. Giants. They were awesome. They had no torches but they glowed with a strange light, and each had a drawn sword in his hand. Who were they?"

Instinctively the missionary knew. He and his wife had prayed for protection, and God had sent His angels. The missionary also recognized that this was a teachable moment for the new convert. "Let me explain what you saw," Patton said as he opened his Bible to Second Kings, Chapter 6. He read the biblical account of the time that the king of Aram sent his army to capture the prophet Elisha. During the night the army surrounded the place where Elisha was. In the morning, Elisha's helper saw that they were surrounded by an army with horses and chariots.

"What shall we do?" the man asked in fear.

"'Don't be afraid,' the prophet answered. Those who are with us are more than those who are with them.' And Elisha prayed, 'O Lord, open his eyes so he may see.' Then the Lord opened the servant's eyes, and he looked and saw the hills full of horses and chariots of fire all around Elisha" (2 Kings 6:16-17).

ANGELS WITH NIGHTSTICKS

JOAN WESTER ANDERSON

Steven Rogers was a rookie officer in the Nutley, New Jersey, police department in 1977 when he was assigned to be partners with Phil. Not only was Phil older and wiser, he was also an outspoken Christian. For the impulsive and sometimes rebellious Steve, Phil became a role model. Daily, before their shift, the two men would pray or read from the Bible, often reciting the Ninety-first Psalm, the one that commits us to God's care and summons angels when we are in danger.

Nutley had a growing problem. Recreational areas were being overrun with teenagers drinking, taking drugs and vandalizing property. Police knew where the kids congregated, but whenever they raided the gatherings, most slipped away and could not be found. Apparently the teens had a hideout, but where? None of the police officers had been able to find it.

One day Steve and Phil were assigned to plainclothes duty. They were to dress like the kids and, it was hoped, discover their hideout and the source of their drugs. That night they stationed themselves in a secluded wooded area and watched the young people fighting, cursing and destroying property.

"What I saw sickened me," Steve relates. "I realized we were not dealing with a few kids 'having fun,' but with many who were hard-core drug addicts with minds out of control. Many were invoking Charles Manson or performing obscene acts. If this behavior spread, it could threaten the whole city."

The main source of the drugs, it appeared, was a young man the officers dubbed Mr. Big because of his apparent emotional hold on the group.

The next day the officers went to the scene of the gathering, prayed for guidance and began to check it inch by inch. They soon came across a well-worn path covered with branches. The path led to a cleverly concealed cave. Inside, the officers found pills, liquor, pornographic material and marijuana. Here was where so many young people eluded the police. That night, they decided, they would raid the cave.

Before their shift, they requested extra backup, but they were told they were on their own. How could two officers handle a bunch of aggressive kids all alone? Once again, the men prayed the Ninety-first Psalm. Then they strolled toward the crowd already gathering near a railroad embankment. Mr. Big was there, they noted. "We wanted to apprehend him first, because we felt so many of the kids would discontinue their illegal activities if he wasn't around," Steve explains.

But as they approached, a girl recognized them. "Cops!" she screamed. The crowd scattered. Steve and Phil went after the girl, caught her and called for a backup squad. By now some of the others, they knew, would be hidden in the cave.

Despite the fact that they were hopelessly outnumbered, they found the hidden path and walked boldly into the entrance. "Freeze!" Steve shouted, and not a person in the cave moved. Steve ran his eyes across the group. At least twelve of them. And they had caught Mr. Big!

Phil walked over to Mr. Big and asked for the package he was holding. Meekly the young man handed over a bag of pills. Steve gathered other evidence, read everyone their rights, then stood in bewilderment, staring at the cave floor covered with submissive teens who could have easily overpowered the two officers. Why hadn't they put up a fight?

The van pulled up, and as they led the prisoners out of the cave, Steve turned to Mr. Big. "Why didn't you or any of the others try to attack us when we came in?"

"You think I'm crazy or something?" Mr. Big asked. "There were at least twenty guys in blue uniforms, and it would have been stupid to think of fighting and running."

"Twenty? No, there were just two of us."

"Yeah?" Mr. Big called to another young prisoner. "Belinda, how many cops came into the cave?"

Belinda shrugged. "At least twenty-five."

It was then that Steve remembered the words he and Phil recited so faithfully:

"You will not fear the terror of night . . . . for he will command his angels concerning you" (Psalm 91:5, 11).

Within nine months from the time Steve and Phil had been assigned to this special duty, they made two hundred and fifty arrests—more than the department's annual total. Former hangouts of drug addicts and vandals were deserted, and Nutley neighborhoods flourished. Whenever anyone complimented the officers on their accomplishments, they gave credit to Jesus for protecting them and helping them solve the crimes.

Jesus . . . and a very special squad in blue.

THE ANGEL CUSTOMERS

ROBERT STRAND

Robert Today owns an over-the-road transport company, but before he got into the trucking business he had purchased a sporting goods store. In the beginning he was the lone employee. The store happened to be in an out-of-the-way part of town, sort of isolated, by itself.

One day, while expressing his concerns to his pastor, the idea struck him to ask the pastor and some of the elders to come over and pray for the protection of his store. They also prayed that anyone who came to buy a gun for the wrong purposes would not be able to do so.

One afternoon a very tough, rough-looking character entered the store to buy a gun. Through the storefront window Robert saw that this man was accompanied by six or seven other equally tough-looking men on motorcycles now parked in front. Immediately Robert sensed that this man did not have good intentions for purchasing a gun. So he refused to sell any guns or ammunition. The man left in an angry huff, jumped on his bike, motioned for the others to follow, made an obscene gesture through the window at Robert and pealed out of the parking lot with tires squealing and pipes roaring.

The next morning this same man returned with his gang but didn't enter the store. They simply began circling the store on their bikes, no doubt with the intent of intimidating Robert. They kept up the harassment most of the day. They would drive out of the lot and return again in a few minutes to circle the store again. All the while they would stare through the front window. Robert, alone in the store, began to pray. "Lord, help me. Please send Your angels to protect me and keep the store safe from any harm."

After several hours of this harassment the leather-jacketed gang drove out of the lot . . . and never returned again!

Later, one of Robert's regular customers dropped by the store to visit. He mentioned that he'd been by earlier in the day but hadn't bothered to come in. Robert asked him why he hadn't.

"Well, because the inside of your store was packed full of customers. I knew you'd be so busy you wouldn't have time to visit with me," he replied.

Yet . . . no one had been in the store at any time that day!

ANGEL IN A BULLS JACKET

Kathy Oldaker

The rumbling of a garbage truck awoke me before seven o'clock Saturday morning in the garage apartment my ten-year-old son and I called home. A messy divorce had left me struggling financially, and I was forced to move with Levi into a less-than-desirable part of town. Drug dealers loitered out front late into the night.

God, will You be able to keep us safe here? I worried.

I nearly jumped out of my skin when I heard banging on the front door. *Who could it be so early?* I threw on a sweat suit and unlocked the door, opening it only partway. There stood a hulking teenager wearing a leather Chicago Bulls jacket. "Yes?" I asked warily.

"Lady, you got a bad gas leak!" I opened the door a bit wider and stuck my head out. The stench of natural gas was overpowering, and I covered my mouth and nose to keep from gagging. "You gotta get out," he said. His deep brown eyes pleaded with me. "The whole place could blow."

"Levi!" I ran to his bedroom. "Wake up," I said, shaking him.

"Mom, it's Saturday," he groaned. "No school."

"Honey, there's a gas leak. We've got to get out of here. Now!" I tossed him a pair of jeans, and he dressed quickly while I grabbed the cordless phone. We rushed outside, where the young man in the Bulls jacket was waiting. "It's gonna be okay," he said. "Call nine-one-one." Of course! I was wasting time. The fumes were growing stronger by the minute.

I dialed. "Emergency," I said to the operator, giving all the information. Help was on the way. "We'll be fine now," I assured the young man, but he stayed to watch the street fill with fire trucks and police cars.

I was called over to answer questions while the rescuers shut the gas off and checked the area. One firefighter came out of the garage with a sniffer, a device that detects flammable vapors in the air. "The gas meter's punctured," he said, trying to catch his breath. "It's lucky you woke up when you did, ma'am." The young man who'd warned me was leaning on our car talking to Levi. There are some good people around here too, I realized, walking over to join them.

"Time to get going," the young man said. "Later, Levi. Take care of your mom." He shook my hand and walked down the street. "Come back anytime," I called after him, waving.

The firefighter in charge told us it was safe to go back inside. "That young man probably saved our lives," I said. The fireman stared at me blankly. "The one who was with my son and me," I added. "You saw him." The crew looked at one another uncomfortably. I tried again. "He was over six feet tall, a black kid in his late teens, wearing a Bulls jacket."

"I'm a Bulls fan," one of the policemen said. "I'd have noticed a kid in a Bulls jacket." "We didn't see any teenagers around here," another officer insisted. "Just you two. And you're darned lucky you got out when you did." I stood in the midst of the dispersing crowd, trying to make sense of what had happened.

Levi took my hand. "I saw him, Mom, so don't worry," he said. And for the first time in ages, I promised God I'd try not to.

MOUNTAINTOP EXPERIENCE

PETER SHOCKEY

Sometimes being high atop a mountain can make you feel closer to God. A young college student named Jocelyn Veile went on a mission retreat to the mountain ranges of Uruguay. On top of one of those mountains, in a strange landscape so far from home, Jocelyn had a memorable and life-changing experience.

Jocelyn leaned back carefully on a boulder. Squinting into the afternoon sun, she surveyed the rough and rocky terrain below. What a day it had been. For the last few hours she and a friend, along with a group of other students, had actually been *climbing a mountain* in Uruguay. *Oh, the stories I'll have to tell,* she mused. It was all pretty high adventure for such a young lady. But, as she and her partner caught their breath, they decided it was probably time to begin the journey back down.

Suddenly, to their horror, she and her friend looked out just in time to see that the bus that had brought them there, along with the rest of their group, was pulling away. Jocelyn recalls, "We didn't know if they had left anybody there to find us. We didn't know if they even knew that we were there." Panic set in and tears filled the young girls' eyes. "We were both really scared," she says. It was in this moment of distress that both girls reached deep down inside for a strength more powerful than fear—their faith in God. "To try to keep ourselves from going too crazy, we started praying," Jocelyn says. "And we started singing praise songs."

Trusting that God would take care of them, they found the courage to begin their long descent down the mountain. At first, they attempted to climb down, much in the same way as they had climbed up, but this proved to be treacherous and difficult. They finally resorted to sitting on the rocks and scooting themselves forward, somewhat like a child on a slide. It was slow going, but they felt as if this would eventually get them to the bottom.

After sliding down in this rather awkward manner for about half and hour, a native man appeared before them, far off the beaten path. "He was a young man," Jocelyn explains, "and my friend and I thought, *Oh, good! Finally somebody who can show us the way down.*"

Excitedly, the girls began waving and calling out to the man. One of the few Spanish words they knew was Ayuda, which means "help." Jocelyn remembers, "Over and over we were yelling, '*Ayuda, Ayuda!*' and pointing down and crying and screaming." Without a word, the man calmly took both the girls' hands and began leading them to the left. Jocelyn and her friend immediately froze in their tracks. "No, *that* way!" the girls cried, again gesturing down the mountain. "*Ayuda, ayuda,*" they said, trying desperately to make their rescuer understand their wishes. He nodded confidently and once again took their hands and began leading them to the left.

Reluctantly, the girls followed. At least the path that he was showing them was a bit easier than scooting down the mountain the way they had been. After a short time and much to the girls' relief, the trio began descending the mountain. Jocelyn recalls thinking, "Well, finally he's figured out what we want here, and he's showing us the way to the bottom."

When at last they made it safely to the parking lot, the girls were glad to find they had not been forgotten. "The group had left a translator and my mother there for us," Jocelyn says.

It was then that their native guide motioned to the girls. Looking up at the mountain, he pointed to the spot where he had found them. Jocelyn and her friend were horrified when they realized they had been only a few feet away from going over a cliff! "When we saw that, we both just kind of lost it," Jocelyn says.

Appreciation for this stranger's kindness filled the girls' hearts. He had literally saved their lives. They realized at that moment that he had been Heaven-sent. How else could they explain the fact that this man had appeared from out of nowhere to lead them down the mountain?

As they walked to the car, Jocelyn pondered this question. Suddenly she realized the man was no longer with them. She recalls, "We took a few steps, turned around, and he was gone." They quickly scanned the area, but their rescuer had completely disappeared. Searching for any trace of their guide, they looked for clues in the soft sand. "There were no footprints," Jocelyn explains. "We could see our footprints in the sand, but his had simply ended."

MISSED OVERALLS

SAM GRAHAM HUMPHREYS

We used to live on a small farm in rural Connecticut. One day I was walking with my three preschool-age sons down the many paths that wove through the woods and pastures surrounding our farm. It had been a wonderful afternoon, and I think we were all a little giddy with the sense of "rightness" in our world. My second son, who was about three years old at the time was dashing a few feet forward and running back like a puppy when I called.

As we approached our large pond, I held tightly to their little hands, knowing that a disaster takes only a second. Maybe it was those few moments of physical restraint that caused him to break away from me once we were safely past the water. At any rate, he scampered off giggling. I could hear him and I could see occasional flashes of the bright red and yellow stripes on his shirt through the bends in the path and the breaks in the trees. At first, when he did not return at my call, I was only mildly concerned, for we knew these paths well, and I could hear that he was not too far ahead. Nevertheless, I wanted to catch up to him quickly. Tucking the baby under one arm and taking a firmer grip on my oldest son, I walked with a faster, more determined stride.

Abruptly my wayward son's giggling veered off in a direction I didn't anticipate.

I paused just long enough to be certain of what I was hearing before scooping my four-year-old up and running toward the sounds. My middle boy, without questions, was taking a less frequently traveled path that eventually made its way up a very steep hill into a horse pasture. I felt my panic rising. Scanning quickly as I reached the foot of the hill, my heart crashed to my toes; there was my boy scrambling like a little mountain goat about halfway up. I placed the baby's hand in that of my oldest son and admonished them to stay put before racing up the hill. It was hard to believe such a little guy could move so fast. Urging him to stop the whole time, I slipped, slid and clambered, all at the same time.

Suddenly, I heard the faint yet unmistakable sound of hoof beats. Someone was riding very near us. It was not unusual for riders to bring the horses down this incline for it was a shortcut to the pond. I also knew that because they were certainly not expecting my son to pop up over the edge, they would never be able to stop the horses in time.

Heart pounding, I doubled my efforts, praying all the while that I would reach him. It was no specific prayer, just, "Please God, please God" over and over. Everything happened at once. I lunged in a last desperate attempt to grab the back of his overalls just as he crested the hill. To my absolute horror and disbelief, I missed and fell with a crash inches from my child. Helplessly I watched, anticipating disaster. Suddenly my son flew backward away from me and landed on his bottom with a dusty thump. The rider tried frantically to stop her horse, which was now pawing and rearing exactly where my son had been only seconds before. Unaware of what had nearly happened, my beloved child turned to me accusingly and scolded, "Mama, you didn't have to pull so hard. That hurt."

I scooped him up into a teary embrace and held him tight, despite his struggles to get loose, until my heart stopped pounding. The rider, her horse under control, and I gazed at each other in amazement. What exactly had happened? I hadn't touched him. There was only one possible answer. I know the guardian angels I heard of as a child are looking out for this new generation just as they always have. When I look at my son today, nineteen years old and quite an amazing young man, I still get a catch in my throat when I think of what might have happened without that moment of divine intervention.

MIRACLE AT CHRISTMAS

JOAN WESTER ANDERSON

I n 1955, Emilie Long's husband, a career Army officer, left active duty and found a consulting job that involved traveling about twenty days a month. Emilie and their three school-age children moved to a hilltop dwelling in New England where Emilie's parents lived. "They were elderly and needed as much care as the children," Emilie says. It was a busy time for her.

Emilie had enjoyed being a military wife, but she was looking forward to settling down. Her only regret was that there would be no additions to the Long family. Several years earlier, she had had surgery that would probably prevent another pregnancy. Emilie prayed the doctors were wrong, but she was almost forty, and the possibility of a miracle grew fainter each year.

Emilie hadn't been settled in the new house long when she came down with a fierce virus. It sidelined her for weeks, but when she went to her doctor for a final checkup, she noticed that instead of losing weight during her ordeal, she had actually gained. "The doctor thought I had a tumor," she recalls, "but when he sent me for tests, neither of us could believe it." Emilie was going to have a baby.

In the midst of her joy, however, there was apprehension. No normal delivery was possible, the doctor said. Emilie, already high-risk because of her age, must go to a specialist in another city for a cesarean section. The due date was debatable. December? January? In the 1950s, technology couldn't be more specific. And was the baby healthy or had the virus affected it?

With her husband away much of the time, and several people depending on her, Emilie wondered how she would manage.

Fall turned into winter. Emilie did chores, talked to her husband long-distance, watched over her parents and her children and prayed for God's protection for her unborn baby. But there were times, especially when the house quieted at night and she contemplated the difficult path ahead, when her faith wavered—just a bit.

Christmas vacation from school was about to begin the day Emilie left for an assessment from the specialist. "He was going to do a final X-ray, which should show when the baby would be large enough to deliver," she says. It was cold, and snow had started to fall, but the twenty-mile drive through picturesque New England towns was uneventful. But Emilie walked out of the doctor's office right into a blizzard.

Her first thought was of her children. Her parents could care for them only so long without needing help themselves. The sooner she reached home, the better. But the roads were treacherous now. What about her own safety and the baby's? What if she crashed or slid into a ditch? Would anyone find her? Once again she felt that terrible isolation. If only she wasn't so alone!

The journey seemed to take hours. Emilie prayed nonstop, her muscles aching as she struggled to keep the car on the road and to see through the whirling flakes. There was little traffic, but as she approached the last mile, she realized the incline was too slippery. She turned toward a longer, but less steep back route.

Carefully Emilie maneuvered up the back road, slow enough to keep traction (and to stop if any cars approached), but fast enough to prevent skidding or getting stuck. There was one right turn to make, then the final slope. The snow was icing, thick under her wheels. Emilie turned, increased speed, spun out and stalled.

Oh, dear God.... She was stuck now, with visibility almost nil and a steep hill in front of her. Perhaps she could climb it on foot. But the abandoned car would be a hazard to any unsuspecting motorist. There was sand in the trunk. Should she try to spread it or to dig herself out? Emilie thought of the shovel and the strain digging would put on her already-exhausted body. But what else could she do?

Leaving the engine idling, she opened the door, then stopped in surprise. A tall man was making his way across the road toward her. He wore a long, dark-gray overcoat, and his hat was pulled over his eyes against the blowing snow. A station wagon stood just behind him, facing her. It was strange that she hadn't seen or heard it until now.

"Stay in the car!" the man called to Emilie. "I'll get you out!" His voice brooked no argument, and Emilie did as she was told.

The man went behind her car, and in a minute she felt it begin to move, climbing the hill easily through the deepening drifts. How incredibly strong he was, Emilie thought, to push the car so quickly. She couldn't see him in her rearview mirror, but when she had reached the top, she braked, opened the window and leaned out to shout her thanks.

But she saw no station wagon. Nor was a helpful figure standing behind her, waving her on. Emilie's bewildered gaze fell on the snowy road next to her car. Soon the plows would clear a path for the evening commuters. But now, not a track or footprint marred the white blanket, even though the station wagon must have driven toward her, past this very spot.

The real Christmas arrived for the Longs when baby Peter did, just a few weeks after December 25. And as Emilie held her small miracle in her arms, she gave silent thanks. She had thought she was alone, but she knew better now. Like another mother from a long-ago time, she had gone through a perilous journey and placed her trust in God. And He had sent angels to guard her in all her ways.

TWO LESSONS ON ANGELS

DAVID MITCHELL

Angels were always mysterious and mythical to me in my early days as a minister. An elderly clergyman once spoke critically of Sir Basil Spence's angels depicted on the huge glass doors of the postwar, reconstructed Coventry Cathedral.

"Who's ever seen an angel like that?" he asked mockingly.

"Who's ever seen an angel?" I replied.

Well, I have learned a lot since then. I have met people who have seen angels and could describe their appearance and relay their words. And I have seen an angel at work, though he remained invisible. It happened like this.

Our daughter Helen was five years old at the time. Delphine and I, with our four young children, were on a post-Easter vacation in the English county of Gloucestershire. Delphine's mother, who was also with us, stopped to talk with someone and, while we were waiting, Helen drifted away to the vacant parking lot of an ancient stone inn.

Watching her closely, I suddenly saw her stumble forward, her head and arms flying backward as if she had been shoved abruptly from behind.

"Daddy, someone pushed me!" she cried, running toward me and clinging to my leg, Just then, a huge stone from the inn's centuries-old chimney broke loose and crashed down on the very spot where Helen had been standing just a few seconds before.

Every skeptical grain in my soul was swept away in that moment. I knew what I had seen with my own eyes.

Some time later I had an opportunity to relate this story.

It was November 1965, and the rain was sheeting down as a west wind came driving up the English Channel. Seven men had gathered for fellowship in the vestry of St. Aidan's Church in Ernesettle, a suburb of Plymouth, Devon. The church served a parish of about six thousand people living in a postwar municipal development.

"Vicar," said the stocky ex-petty officer Vic Selway, "do you believe in angels?" I replied that I certainly did and recounted the story I have just told you. "I believe there are many occasions when angels intervene for God's children, just as it says in Hebrews 1:14: 'Are not all angels ministering spirits sent to serve those who will inherit salvation?'"

The men sat quietly for a moment or two, then began recounting their own personal stories that could possibly be explained by the presence of angels. The most memorable was that of Fred Train.

Fred was a warm, friendly man who seemed to know everyone. His face was always alight with a big smile. He was strong, yet gentle, and seemed to spend all his spare time serving others.

Not only was he a pillar of strength in the church, he also ran a large city-sponsored youth group in the park behind my vicarage. I knew Fred had a powerful influence on many youngsters who would probably not have been caught dead in a church.

"It was like this, "he said. "During the war I served on a destroyer and got pretty close to all the men. There wasn't a man on that ship I didn't know." *I can understand that,* I thought. *Fred is that kind of man.*

"The terrible day came," Fred continued, "when we were torpedoed in the Atlantic. The order came to abandon ship. She was listing sharply. I was sliding down the deck toward my lifeboat station when a matelot [sailor] with a big black beard grabbed me.

"'Fred,' he said, 'you've forgotten your grandfather's Bible!' My granddad had given me his Bible in the hope that I would read it. I never had. In fact, I never even opened it. But I did treasure it and kept it tucked away in my locker. So, before I knew what I was doing, I found myself scrambling back up the deck to get the Bible.

"When I got back to the lifeboat station, my boat had gone. I had just time enough to pile into the last lifeboat. We were pulling away from the ship when another torpedo passed close by us and hit a lifeboat already in the water. It was blown to smithereens. Vicar," he continued, "that was the boat I was supposed to have been in."

Fred paused briefly.

"The funny thing is that not one member of the crew knew I had a Bible. And," Fred swallowed and tears glistened in his eyes, "I had never seen that sailor before in my life!"

www.guidepostsbooks.com

Series Editor: Patricia S. Klein

Designed by Monica Elias

Jacket photo courtesy of Photodisc

Typeset by Composition Technologies, Inc.

Typists: Carla Collins, Rachel Eden and Judith Silvio

Printed in the United States of America

This original Guideposts Book was created by the Book and Inspirational Media Division of the company that publishes *Guideposts*, a monthly magazine filled with true stories of hope and inspiration.

Guideposts is available by subscription. All you have to do is write to Guideposts, 39 Seminary Hill Road, Carmel, New York 10512. When you subscribe, each month you can count on receiving exciting new evidence of God's presence, His guidance and His limitless love for all of us.

Guideposts Books are available on the World Wide Web at www.guidepostsbooks.com. Follow our popular book of devotionals, *Daily Guideposts*, and read excerpts from some of our best-selling books. You can also send prayer requests to our Monday morning Prayer Fellowship and read stories from recent issues of our magazines, *Guideposts*, *Angels on Earth*, and *Guideposts for Teens*.